·PIER 21·

AN ILLUSTRATED HISTORY OF CANADA'S GATEWAY

Alexa Thompson and Debi van de Wiel

NIMBUS
PUBLISHING LTD

TROOPSHIP "NIEUW AMSTERDAM" ARRIVING AT HALIFAX N.S. SEP. 29TH 1945

Nimbus Publishing Limited
PO Box 9166
Halifax, NS   B3K 5M8
(902) 455-4286

Printed and bound in Canada

Design: Arthur Carter, Paragon Design Group

Cover: S.S. *Olympic* tied up at Pier 21. The *Olympic* was used as a troop carrier during World War One and as a passenger ship between the wars.

Title page: The *Nieuw Amsterdam* brings
troops home to Halifax in September 1945.

National Library of Canada Cataloguing in Publication

Thompson, Alexa
Pier 21 : an illustrated history of Canada's gateway /
Alexa Thompson, Debi van de Wiel.

ISBN 1-55109-397-9

1. Ports of entry—Nova Scotia—Halifax—History. 2. Canada—Emigration and immigration—History—20th century. 3. Immigrants—Canada—History—20th century. I. van de Wiel, Debi, 1952- II. Title.

JV7225.T46 2002   325.71   C2002-902188-X

Canadä   The Canada Council | Le Conseil des Arts
            for the Arts | du Canada

We acknowledge the financial support of the Government of Canada through the Book Publishing Industry Development Program (BPIDP) and the Canada Council for our publishing activities.

Dedicated to the memory of Her Majesty Queen Elizabeth, the Queen Mother, 1900-2002

Her Majesty Queen Elizabeth waves graciously as she and King George VI board the *Empress of Britain* at Pier 21 in Halifax, Nova Scotia in June 1939.

Contents

Chapter One:
18th- and 19th-Century Halifax 1

Chapter Two:
Pier 2—At Peace and War 9

Chapter Three:
Pier 21—Between the Wars 31

Chapter Four:
Pier 21 during World War Two 43

Chapter Five:
Canada's Merchant Marines 65

Chapter Six:
Hosting British Guest Children 77

Chapter Seven:
War Brides 83

Chapter Eight:
Pier 21's Distinguished Voluntary Organizations 97

Chapter Nine:
Refugees and Displaced Persons—The Post-war Years 109

Chapter Ten:
New Immigrants 117

Chapter Eleven:
Pier 21 Today 127

Image Sources 140

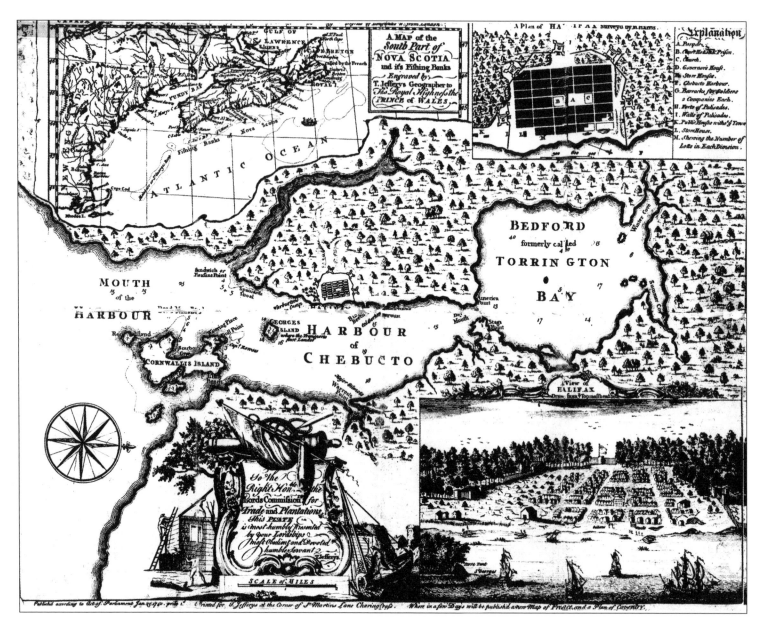

Map of Halifax Harbour (Harbour of Chebucto) and the Bedford Basin (Torrington Bay) as it appeared in *Gentleman's Magazine*, January 1750, just a few months after the city was founded (June 21, 1749).

CHAPTER ONE

18th- and 19th-Century Halifax

"Halifax is the best in the world, and by its natural form, and an island at its entrance, is capable of being well defended by fortifications."
—Otis Little, First Attorney General and Commissonaire of Stores (c. 1750.)

Immigrants have been attracted to Halifax Harbour for thousands of years. Archaeological evidence of Mi'kmaq summer camps along the Bedford Basin places them on the eastern continent hundreds of years before the first Europeans arrived in North America, but the story of Halifax and the hundreds of thousands of immigrants who have passed this way begins in 1749 with Colonel Edward Cornwallis.

For 36 years, since the signing of the Treaty of Utrecht between Great Britain and France in 1713, there had been an uneasy peace in the British colony of Nova Scotia. At that time the colony included what is today the provinces of New Brunswick and Nova Scotia, but not Cape Breton Island, which remained in the hands of the French. The French presence on Cape Breton—and especially the huge fortress at Louisbourg—as well as marauding bands of Acadians and Mi'kmaq created fear among English settlers. The colonial capital at Annapolis Royal was considered too far away to offer real protection against an invasion of ships from Louisbourg. And disturbances between English and French dissenters on the Isthmus of Chignecto, near what is today the Nova Scotia-New Brunswick border, added to the uneasiness. Colonel Cornwallis was charged with finding a site for a new capital. He chose Halifax, with its deep, natural harbour and ease of defence. A hill overlooking the harbour and a string of islands at its mouth meant that fortifications could be built to protect the town and its people from attack both overland and by sea.

Cornwallis, Halifax's first governor, arrived with shiploads of soldiers, sailors, and craftsmen to build a garrison on what is today Citadel Hill. He named the town Halifax after his patron, George Montagu Dunk, second Earl of Halifax. The artisans and their families remained, and soon were joined by other immigrants lured by incentives offered by Lord Halifax—free passage, land grants, ammunition, tools and materials, and food to last a year. To those sickened by poverty or fleeing religious or political persecution in Europe, Halifax must have been very appealing. Within a year, 353 pilgrims from Plymouth in Cornwall had arrived aboard the *Alderney* on the Dartmouth side of the harbour. And in Halifax, about 300 German Protestants lingered, waiting for resettlement on farms under the protection of the fortified town of Lunenburg being built on Nova Scotia's south shore. The Germans found resettling particularly difficult since they did not speak English and were unfamiliar with British ways.

By the end of the 1750s, Halifax was overflowing with soldiers, sailors, and other military personnel readying for a siege of Fortress Louisbourg. The navel dockyards, with facilities to repair ships, opened in 1759. Within twenty years, the town was handling its first refugees as United Empire Loyalists fled the American War of Independence and streamed into Halifax. Among them were free Blacks, who settled in areas throughout the

1759 sketch of Halifax Harbour from the southeast slope of Citadel Hill. Of particular interest is the Great Pontack Inn (left side of the sketch), located at the corner of Duke and Water streets, and the governor's summer farm, now the site of Government House on Barrington Street.

The evacuation of the city of Boston by General Charles Cornwallis and his troops during the American War of Independence.

province, including the Preston area, slightly east of Dartmouth. So many immigrants and refugees arrived that, by 1783, Halifax could no longer house all its destitute.

Despite the garrison at the Citadel, Halifax was still considered vulnerable to attack, particularly by privateers or American ships of war. It fell to Edward, Duke of Kent, during his tenure as governor at the turn of the nineteenth century, to shore up defences. He ringed the harbour with fortifications from Hamlin Point on the east side, across the islands of Georges and MacNabs, to York Redoubt on the west entrance.

Now a safe haven, Halifax became a bustling seaport during the early 1800s. Tradesmen mingled with sailors, immigrants with privateers, businessmen with pickpockets, prostitutes, and other characters. Boatyards, chandlers, warehouses, and banks sprang up at what is today Historic Properties. It was a prosperous time. Newspapers flourished. Universities were founded—the oldest, the University of King's College, in 1789, followed by Saint Mary's School for Boys (later Saint Mary's University) in 1802 and Dalhousie University in 1820. Well-educated Haligonians met in coffee shops to discuss business and politics. In the midst of all this, Joseph Howe, politician and owner of the influential newspaper *The Novascotian*, led the colony in becoming the first seat of responsible government in British North America in 1848.

With prosperity came a wealthier class of immigrant. Earlier settlers had included Europe's most impoverished: from the city slums, Highland crofters clearing off their lands; Irish workers facing starvation during repeated famines; Blacks, both free and enslaved; West Indians, especially Jamaicans; and Loyalists, fleeing both the American Revolution and the War of 1812. Many of those Loyalists found it difficult to adjust. A number had been important members of their local communities—doctors, lawyers, teachers, men of commerce. They left behind homes and often relatives who had sided with the Americans in the two wars. But as the century progressed, a middle class settled in Halifax. They started banks, opened factories, and built Victorian-styled homes in the south end of Halifax, upwind of their factory furnaces.

In the north end lived the immigrant working classes—refugees from European wars, African conflicts, and Asian poverty. Often they arrived aboard derelict ships. As the *Acadian Recorder* wrote in 1839: "the vessels used in transport of immigrants across the Atlantic were fit only for firewood."

At the very tip of the north end of the peninsula, there was Africville, founded by Black United Empire Loyalists. Promised freedom and land in Nova Scotia, they found limited freedom and the poorest of land. But through deep attachment to their community and to their culture they survived.

Throughout the century, immigrants continued to pour into Halifax: French prisoners of war, gold prospectors lured by the promise of gold along the Eastern Shore, West Indians seeking a new homeland. In the 1840s, driven by potato crop failures and repeated famine, 400,000 Irish men, women, and children arrived in Canada—a few thousand of whom elected to settle in the Maritime region. These immigrants brought with them their culture, their languages, and their religions. Very soon ethnic societies sprang up. Banquets were held for the Irish on St. Patrick's Day, for the English on St. George's Day, and for the Scots on St. Andrew's Day. The Scots created the North British and Highland Societies and African immigrants founded Slave Emancipation Day.

By 1864, Halifax had its own police force, although the military remained on hand to quell riots or other acts of violence. And in 1869, just two years after Confederation, the first Immigration Act was established under federal rather than colonial jurisdiction. Eight centres, including Halifax, were officially designated to receive and process immigrants. In 1881, the city was declared a port of entry to Canada.

Canada opened its doors to immigrants and they flooded in. All but criminals, the destitute, and those with either physical or mental disabilities were welcomed. Some restrictions were placed on the number of Asian immigrants allowed entry as well. In the last quarter of the nineteenth century, there were marked changes in where immigrants settled. Fewer stayed in Halifax or even Nova Scotia. The Intercolonial Railway, a condition of Confederation, linked the rail-line between Halifax and Truro with the line between Rivière du Loup and Montreal. Many immigrants now disembarked in Halifax, were processed through immigration, then boarded a train for central and western Canada.

With the opening up of the Canadian west and with larger and swifter steamships replacing the old sailing ships, the number of immigrants pouring through the terminals in Halifax was becoming unwieldy. It was obvious that there was a critical need for a single terminal large enough to receive and process the volume of immigrants.

View of the Halifax waterfront from the Dartmouth shore (circa 1853). The mill to the left, known as The Red Mill, was a water-driven grist mill that adjoined an eighteenth-century windmill built by James Munn. The mill was torn down in 1901 to make way for a tennis court. All that remains today is the name—Windmill Road.

The Departure of the Emigrants' Ship.

The emigrants at dinner amid-ships.

From the *London Illustrated News*. Life at sea for nineteenth-century immigrants was probably a lot more uncomfortable than these two views suggest. The first depicts immigrants crowded on deck as the ship prepares to embark for the New World. Passengers usually preferred to remain on deck rather than descend to the holds, which were often extremely crowded and riddled with disease—hardly the pleasant scene of passengers enjoying a meal presented in the image above. These images were probably produced to encourage emigration.

Construction of Pier 2. Begun in the 1880s, the pier was finally destroyed after the building was condemned nearly a century later. This rare photograph from the Tom Connors Collection is dated November 4, 1911.

CHAPTER TWO

Pier 2—At Peace and War

"Our greatest adjustment to life in Canada was to learn English. Other Polish people, already living there were very helpful and translated for us. We also had a Polish/English dictionary and we learned enough English to get by. We found people in Canada worked very hard and wanted to prosper."
—Polish immigrant, circa early 1900s

By the end of the 1800s, Halifax was struggling to meet the demands of immigrants. Ocean liners had replaced steamships such as the Cunard Steamship Company, Allan Line, Furness Withy Company, and other smaller ones. Liners could carry even greater numbers of immigrants. Between 1895 and 1906, over 150,000 arrived in Halifax; most of them were promised work in the Canadian west, where there was a desperate shortage of skilled farm labourers.

In addition, 95,000 "home children," children and adolescents from the slums and orphanages of England, were helped to find a new life in Canada. Agencies in both countries handled the processing of these young people and found families to sponsor them. Boys were needed to work on farms while girls went into domestic service.

These numbers swelled by between two and four thousand, not only because of the military personnel and their families stationed in Halifax, but also because of the prostitutes, pickpockets, and other petty criminal such a presence attracted. Halifax was buckling under the strain.

It was obvious as early as the 1870s that the city desperately needed one facility equipped to handle all new immigrants, and that the facility should abut the Intercolonial Railway (renamed Canadian National Railway at the turn of the twentieth century) terminus at the north end, where the railway lines ran from Halifax Harbour to Quebec City. Ottawa recognized the potential of Halifax as a national port. Already a naval facility, the government realized the port could play an important role in times of war and be a gateway for immigrants in times of peace.

Pier 2, the new facility, was built on land owned by Samual Cunard, owner of the Cunard Steamship Company. It was also known as the Deep Water Terminus, a bit of a misnomer since the water here was no deeper than elsewhere in the harbour. But it was a mile closer to the open ocean than other government railway terminals in the North End.

A dispatch in the February 4, 1880 *Journal of Remarkable Occurrences* states: "in the fourteenth and fifteenth years of the Canadian Union the Deep Water Terminus of the Intercolonial Railway at Halifax, N.S. was completed. The work commenced in June 1877."

Within a year of its completion, additions were already being tacked on, such as a shed approximately 546 feet long and 46 feet wide and large enough to store the coal being mined in Nova Scotia. Around 1882 the *Halifax Herald* stated: "when the works now in progress are completed, Halifax will have shipping facilities surpassing those of any other port in the Dominion and indeed, it is said by some, surpassing anything in North America."

Not far ahead, however, disaster lurked. In 1895, a fire raged through the structure, although the pier itself was spared. Reconstruction of the

continued on page 15

Acc. No. 9166.

View from the steeple of Saint Patrick's Roman Catholic Church of the Deep Water Terminus (Pier 2) and the grain elevator in the North End, circa 1900. Although known colloquially as "the Deep Water Terminus," it was no deeper in fact than other parts of the harbour, although it was closer to the harbour entrance than previous government rail-serviced piers.

Early picture of Pier 2 showing the Intercolonial Railway lines in the foreground and Royal Navy warships in the harbour.

A view of the Halifax waterfront looking southeast of Pier 2, circa 1902.

Ships docked at piers 2 and 3, circa 1910.

The S.S. *Parisian* burned and sank at Pier 2 after colliding with the German ship S.S. *Albania*, March 29, 1905. Divers at Pier 2 work on the wreck before refloating it.

buildings, this time in concrete, did not begin until September 1911 and wasn't completed until early 1915, several months after the start of World War One in July 1914.

In the early part of the twentieth century, however, immigrants continued to arrive in great numbers—nearly 2.7 million of them over the pre-war years. Most were British, although others included Eastern European farmers needed in the Canadian west. In 1913 alone, 100,000 immigrants arrived at Pier 2 on 200 steamships. It was becoming obvious that the facility could barely handle the crush.

Proposals were put forth to create another facility to handle the flood of immigrants. The Halifax Board of Trade was determined to provide Halifax with improved terminal facilities for rail transportation. The idea was to extend the railway lines past Pier 2 to the South End of Halifax, where a new terminal would be built—one that could accommodate large ocean liners and help improve commercial shipping. In 1912, the proposal received federal government approval and work began on the railway lines. But before the terminus could be started, war was declared and the plans were shelved.

Focus quickly shifted from immigration to the embarkation of Canadian troops destined for the European war. Pier 2 was taken over by the Department of Militia and Defence because it had the facilities to examine and classify every person who volunteered for Canada's war efforts, and because as many as 600 people could be cleared through the facility every two to three days.

Halifax Ocean Terminals, Halifax, N.S.

Postcard of an artist's concept of the ocean terminus in Halifax. The reverse side, addressed to Miss Porah Begin of Mahone Bay, Nova Scotia, reads: "I am going to send you this card to let you know that I am coming home Saturday with the afternoon tides. Be sure to come to Pier 2 to meet me. Don't forget about the Station—I will have a lot to tell you when I come home from the ship." (February 5, 1919)

Trains brought troops from across Canada to the Pier 2 terminals, where soldiers boarded such ships as the *Mauretania* and S.S. *Olympic*, the sister-ship to the ill-fated *Titanic*. Over 300,000 Canadian troops left for Europe from Pier 2, among them Nova Scotia regiments that included the 25th, 64th, 185th, 193rd, and 219th battalions; the 6th Mounted Rifles; the Royal Canadian Regiment; and the Nova Scotia Highlanders, who left on the S.S. *Olympic*. Convoys gathered in formation in Bedford Basin, and Royal Naval warships were a common sight in the harbour.

Censorship was in effect and, as of September 12, 1914, "all lights in private homes, shops, warehouses, and other buildings must be covered with blinds (Halifax, Dartmouth, and vicinity, including Bedford Basin, the area to Sambro Island and along the Eastern Shore of Halifax). Public buildings, such as restaurants and hotels, had to ensure that no lights from their facilities could be seen out to sea."

Despite strict censorship, rumours and leaks abounded. There were stories about Halifax being a nest of spies, intrigue, and secrets—it must have been an interesting place on the Halifax waterfront in the early days of war. One young guard recalls one night in particular:

"…a heavy fog was drifting in, visibility was zero and familiar objects took on weird shapes. There I was, prodding back and forth with only my rifle for company. Everything was quiet except for the occasional slapping of the waves on the beach below. My thoughts turned to my home in Cape Breton. "Would I get home

The 25th Nova Scotia Regiment being seen off at Pier 2, on May 20, 1915.

Entrance to the Halifax Citadel, founded 1749—reconstructed c.1828

A number of prisoners of war, most of them German or Austrian, were detained in military prisons, either in the Halifax Citadel or at the facility constructed on Melville Island along the Northwest Arm, where the Armdale Yacht Club is today.

Military Prison. Melville Island, Halifax, N.S.

this year? I was thinking probably about our cows, when I heard it. It sounded like a cow chewing her cud, but that was impossible … But there it was again, that dull muffled 'click, click.' I peered into the darkness but could see nothing. I held my breath; someone was coming. And from the beach, where no one was allowed.

"I called 'Halt.' He replied in a language I didn't know and kept on coming. Now was the time for action; I aimed my rifle over his head and fired. Immediately, several soldiers rushed out of the guardhouse and seized him and a parcel that proved to be a bomb!

"Next day my mysterious noise was explained. Our "visitor" had used a pair of wire snippers to cut the barbed wire and get into our camp. The enemy must have thought we slept at night."

Through the upper floor of the transit shed at Pier 2, Canadian soldiers embarked for war over the first four years of its duration, their numbers swelling by the arrival of American troops and more than 50,000 Chinese engaged to work on construction. Accommodation became a serious problem. There were not enough barracks and depots to house the hundreds of thousands of soldiers in transit. Still, lumber was cheap and plentiful, and camps of long wooden huts were quickly erected on the Halifax Commons, Citadel Hill, and along neighbouring Cogswell Street.

At the start of the war, African Nova Scotians could not join up, but within a few years they were enlisted in the 2nd Construction Battalion. Jewish Canadians were equally discouraged from taking part at the front. A number did transfer to camps in Windsor, Nova Scotia, and some were stationed at York Redoubt, which guarded the harbour approach.

Women played an active role on the home front. They were in great demand as volunteers, and numerous ads, such as the following, appeared in local newspapers, urging women to give of their time to the war effort:

"Will you lend your car to returned soldiers? They are here now—seven hundred of them; and the Red Cross Committee plan to give them a drive Sunday afternoon. As before, we appeal to the generosity of car owners. Wonderfully generous has been the response in the past. Will you lend your car, send or bring it Sunday afternoon at 2:30 to Pier 2? Both the Red Cross committee and the returned men will be duly grateful."

Women also took over many of the jobs previously held by men, such as streetcar conductors, postal carriers, and police officers. They had easy access to hospital, legal, and factory work and education programs.

17

Two ocean liners, the *Celtic* and the *Baltic*, tied up near Pier 2. These are two second generation "Big 4-class" White Star liners converted to World War One troop ships. The *Celtic* ran aground near Cobh, Ireland. Attempts to salvage the wreck in 1933 were unsuccessful.

By 1915 Halifax was overflowing with troops preparing to go overseas, construction workers, and newcomers arriving from rural areas to take over jobs vacated by soldiers headed for Europe. Accommodation was hard to come by. In this picture postcard, soldiers are shown housed in wooden huts, built hurriedly to handle the troops amassing in Halifax. The card, dated 1916, is addressed to Miss Edna Langille of Cumberland County, Nova Scotia. It reads: "Dear Friend: Received your letter and oblige for same. H.B."

Undated and unidentified photograph of troops embarking at Pier 2 for World War One.

**World War One hospital ship, possibly the *Morro Castle*. A ship of the same
name burned off the coast of New Jersey in 1934.**

Author and folklorist Dr. Helen Creighton stands beside the troop ship *Minikhada*, **docked at Pier 2 in 1919.**

The S.S. *Olympic*, also one of the boats in Dr. Creighton's collection, converted to a troop carrier. Towards the end of the war, on October 18, 1918, the
Olympic was attacked by a German submarine. The captain turned the ship
around and rammed and sank the sub. After World War One, the *Olympic*
was returned to civilian service but made only one other trip to Halifax,
bringing immigrants to Pier 21 in 1934.

This photograph, taken from a postcard, shows the North End of Halifax from the grain elevator located at the foot of Cornwallis Street. It was taken around 1900 and shows the North End as it would have been before the Halifax Explosion on December 6, 1917, in which the French munitions ship S.S. *Mont Blanc* and the Norwegian relief ship *Imo* collided. The explosion levelled a large section of the North End.

By 1915, Halifax was bustling as soldiers arrived at Pier 2 and convoys amassed in the Bedford Basin. Prisoners of war began to arrive, most either German or Austrian, to be housed either in Citadel Hill or at the prison on Melville Island in the Northwest Arm. As war continued, soldiers began returning to Canada, many of them wounded. Despite medical facilities at Pier 2, Halifax hospitals could not cope with the flood of casualties. In 1917, the Camp Hill Military Hospital was built to cope with emergency. It wasn't long before city hospitals had another disaster on their hands. On December 6, 1917, after a collision with the *Imo* the ammunition ship *Mont Blanc* blew up, levelling most of the north end of Halifax, killing two thousand people and wounding nine thousand more. One survivor wrote: "The ground under Halifax felt like an earthquake had hit. Someone said, 'Buildings collapsed, trapping people; glass and metal flew through the air; it looked like fireballs were being thrown.'" Another recalled: "When the explosion happened, people couldn't remember hearing it—it just happened. There was no escaping. Then came the silence. All around were the dead, the dying, the cries of human voices, and the crackling of fires."

At Pier 2, the reception hospital and clearing depot for the wounded were badly damaged, but, as the *Morning Chronicle* reported on December 13, 1917: "By a fortunate circumstance the last ship load of returned soldiers had been cleared through Pier 2 hospital several days before the accident, otherwise, there might have been heavy casualties in the depot, which was practically empty at the time of the explosion."

The concrete shed at Pier 2 survived the blast better than most nearby buildings, but it did suffer severe structural stress that restricted its ability to handle immigration for the next decade. And for war-weary soldiers returning from war to Pier 2, the sight of the devastated city must have been particularly grim.

Immediately after the war, Pier 2 became a discharge depot and military hospital for returning troops. The upper level still housed hospital facilities divided into wards, administration offices and storerooms, as well as sleeping quarters for staff. At the lower level, hospital trains were loaded with victims. A tuberculosis hospital with massive windows to let in the light, along with kitchens and dining rooms, were placed at one end of the building.

Returning troops faced economic and social conditions that were equally disheartening. Most of the world had been plunged into a recession: work was scarce and unemployment lines long. Tensions were high and Chinese and African Nova Scotians felt the brunt of racism.

Halifax, in particular the building trade, had a bit of a reprieve in 1919 and 1920. Homes to replace those destroyed by the Halifax Explosion were being built in the North End, in what today is known as the Hydrostone. Regardless, Halifax and all of Nova Scotia went through a recession that was to last nearly two decades. The Navy was decimated, left with fewer personnel, two minesweepers, and two destroyers. Only the newly formed Canadian Air Force stayed aloft, making periodic surveys of Halifax. But down at the Halifax Dockyards, hundreds of workers were laid off and many factories, destroyed by the explosion, were never rebuilt. Economic conditions were bleak. Immigration to Nova Scotia all but dried up. Most of those who arrived at Pier 2 moved west or to the United States in search of work. Others, disillusioned and disheartened by what they saw in Canada, returned voluntarily to their homelands or were deported. During the 1920s and 1930s, only 140,000 arrived, almost all of them either British or American citizens.

Camp Hill, Military Hospital, Halifax, N.S.—84

Pier 2 had a military hospital located on its top floor, but by 1917 the facility could no longer cope with the number of wounded soldiers needing medical attention. The Camp Hill Military Hospital was built to cope with the overload. The hospital, located on Veteran's Lane between Robie and Summer streets in Halifax, remains a hospital for veterans.

Outside a train near Pier 2, Russian immigrant children, who fled the revolution, pose as an unidentified conductor looks on (1919). These children were among the first refugees to reach Canada after World War One. They would have been moved to families and homes in other parts of Canada, most likely to work as domestic or farm labourers.

Pier 2 in the 1930s with a steamship docked alongside. Pier 2 was built to serve as a freight and immigration pier for the Intercolonial Railway, and the shed was built by the Department of Railways and Canals specifically for the railway. Tracks ran along each edge of the pier and two additional tracks ran down the centre of the shed, diving it in two. Trains could move in and out of the pier, carrying new immigrants to other parts of Canada or bringing troops to their ships during World War One. The facility was used as a discharge depot during the war, with the lower floor being used to load hospital trains while the upper level housed hospital facilities, including a tuberculosis clinic.

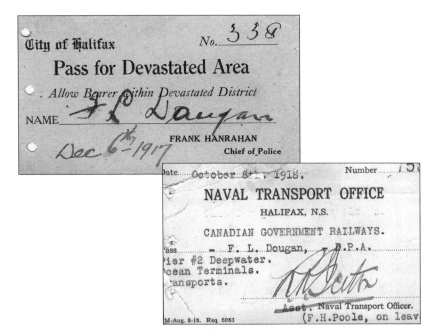

F.L. Dougan appears to have worked for the Canadian Government railways at Pier 2. On December 6, 1917, he was issued a pass that allowed him to enter the devastated north end of the city following that morning's explosion in Halifax Harbour. And ten months later, on October 10, 1918, Dougan was provided with a Naval Transport Office pass. He was still at work at Pier 2 as late as 1935.

Volunteers and church groups were always ready to greet immigrants. In 1919, the Canadian Council of Immigration Women was organized to help immigrant women and provide them with accommodation while they remained in Halifax. The Canadian Red Cross started helping immigrants in 1920. They also tended to sick and wounded soldiers returning home. The Red Cross was joined by a few members of the Roman Catholic Sisters of Service. Many of these women could speak other languages and they would do all they could for the immigrants, even writing grocery lists or sending telegrams to relatives in their homelands. They took care of those in hospitals and detention centres.

Halifax did get some relief during the 1920s. The plans to build a facility and railway terminus in the South End were revisited. New CNR facilities were built and lines extended, and the Department of Immigration opened its new immigrant doorway, Pier 21, in 1928.

Pier 2 didn't quite slip into history. It continued to serve Halifax well as a freight and shipping terminal and remained the largest and busiest structure in the Deep Water Terminus. It could still accommodate the passenger ships of its time and freight moved easily from ships' holds onto trains—some of which pulled up along the length of the pier or passed directly into the shed.

By the end of the 1920s, the demand for a storage facility to handle increased commerce in the Great Lakes region brought about yet another pier refurbishment. This time a warehouse that could store 1.5 million cubic feet of goods and other produce was built. Halifax's future as a seat of commerce looked bright.

But in September 1933 disaster struck again. A fire ravaged the upper storey of Pier 2 with a financial loss exceeding half a million dollars. It looked like a crippling blow to the pier and to the city's shipping industry. However, in just five months and despite contractual squabbles and fierce winter weather, the pier was back to full operational strength. In the words of Harbour Commissioner J.L. Hetherington, "Pier 2 is now elevated to the position better than ever." A ramp allowed vehicular access to the top floor, escalators were added, and plumbing was upgraded. And, no doubt to the delight of stevedores and cargo handlers, a heating system was installed.

Used during World War Two for storage purposes, terminal facilities were taken over by the naval Dockyard in the 1960s. Pier 2's heyday was by then long over. Immigrants no longer crowded its buildings. The oldest significant structure on the Halifax shoreline was torn down in the 1980s, a few years after the buildings were condemned.

View of Pier 2 in the 1970s.

Aerial view of the Halifax Waterfront showing Pier 2 and Pier 21 in the 1970s.

CHAPTER THREE

Pier 21—Between the Wars

"It is here that every immigrant who enters Canada by way of Halifax first sets foot on Canadian soil. It is here that first and perhaps lasting impressions of the new country are made"
—The Open Gateway, Halifax Harbour Commissioners, 1932, in reference to Pier 21

Pier 21 opened with little fanfare as the steamship *Nieuw Amsterdam* docked, with 51 immigrants aboard, on March 28, 1928. The Halifax Harbour Commission, established in 1928, oversaw the completion of ocean terminals and port facilities in the vicinity of Pier 21. Piers, transit sheds, and a grain elevator were built in the south end of Halifax, adjacent to the railway lines.

The new facility was immense, covering an area of about 221,000 square feet. Two storeys high and 600 feet long, it was connected by covered ramps to an annex and to the terminus for the Canadian National Railway (CNR). Immigrants could disembark and board a train for points west without stepping outdoors.

The first floor was designed to handle freight unloaded off the ocean liners. Through the second-floor windows—barred for security—new arrivals could be seen passing through the immigration process. Here one could find a score of offices, including the Canadian Immigration Department, Canada Customs, and the Currency Exchange. There was a reception area for immigrants, a medical clinic, complete with hospital and waiting rooms for those requiring medical examinations, kitchens, cafeterias, and a canteen. Nurseries were set up to care for immigrant children while their parents were being processed, and dormitories for up to 150 guests were available for anyone who needed to stay overnight before moving on. There was even a detention centre that could house ten detainees. It may have been clean and efficient, but Pier 21 was a stark, cold building with an austerity that must have been daunting to many travel-weary immigrants. However, as they entered the facility, new arrivals were greeted by a massive Union Jack—a reassuring sight, especially for the thousands of immigrants from the United Kingdom. Most of those who did pass through the pier during the decade preceding World War Two were wealthy and either British or, to a lesser extent, American.

Passengers disembarking at Pier 21 were led along the gangplank of the second floor to an assembly room. There, they were admitted individually or by family, and taken to offices to undergo medical examinations and immigration interviews. Those who failed either were sent to the Dominion Immigration Agent's Office for another examination. If they failed this one as well, they were housed in the detention centre to await deportation. Others who safely passed the tests proceeded down a hall to collect hand luggage, then along a ramp that connected the Immigration Hall with the annex. In the annex they were able to retrieve their heavy baggage, each piece of which had been carefully checked by custom officials. This area also functioned as a train station, so the processed immigrants could easily transfer to a train going west. According to John Hood, a representative of the people of Pier 21, "it was in the long overtime hours voluntarily spent by seniors and clerks at the ticket windows, and in the personal services to passengers at the baggage-room, in the dining-room

Scale model of Pier 21 in its heyday. Note the walkways from the second floor immigration level across the railway tracks. In this way it was easy for travellers to disembark, go through immigration and board trains for distant parts of Canada.

On March 28, 1928, the *Nieuw Amsterdam* sailed into Halifax Harbour and docked at Pier 21. Although received with little fanfare, this arrival was a historic moment as the *Nieuw Amsterdam* was the first immigrant ship to arrive at the new facility. Seated on the deck is the ship's captain, De Jong (with a Presentation Cane), flanked by immigration, customs, harbour, railway, and steamship officials.

The Nova Scotian and C.N.R. Station, Halifax, Nova Scotia, Canada.—31.

The Nova Scotian hotel was built adjacent to Pier 21 and the railway terminus so that immigrants would have a place to stay between disembarking and boarding trains for other parts of Canada. Most immigrants, however, could not afford the luxury of the hotel and stayed instead in the Pier 21 dormitories. The two-storey facility can be seen at left, with a ship at dock. The tunnels from the pier led to the annex of the Canadian National Railway Station.

It would seem that F.L. Dougan enjoyed his work with the Halifax Harbour Commission. Dockyard passes for visits in 1917 (at the time of the Halifax Explosion), 1918, and 1935 survive.

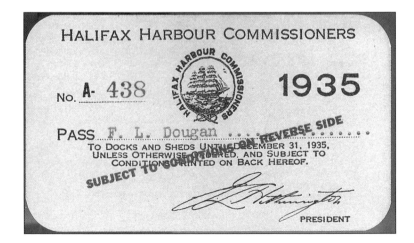

HALIFAX HARBOUR COMMISSIONERS

No. A- 438

1935

PASS F. L. Dougan ....ON REVERSE SIDE

TO DOCKS AND SHEDS UNTIL DECEMBER 31, 1935, UNLESS OTHERWISE ORDERED, AND SUBJECT TO CONDITIONS PRINTED ON BACK HEREOF.

SUBJECT TO

PRESIDENT

and at the money exchange bureau, at the railway, that difficulties were smoothed out. All passengers were watched over with great care and compassion…."

In the first couple of years of operation, Pier 21 handled between 42,000 and 45,000 immigrants. The number dropped to less than half that during the first full year of the Depression, with only 20,809 new arrivals in 1930. For the rest of the decade, immigration was dismal with between 1,700 and 3,000 arriving annually.

As the world sank further into the Depression, Halifax tried to jump-start an economic boom based on tourism. When cars and buses replaced horses, the wealthy were able to travel farther. Department stores such as Eaton's and Simpson's and elegant hotels such as The Lord Nelson and the Nova Scotian were built. Schooner races were all the rage and Nova Scotians flocked to watch the Lunenburg-built *Bluenose* win its races. One of the more colourful events along the waterfront was the arrival of "The Lady Boats," sleek, white ships each named for the wives of British naval admirals.

In the mid-1920s, Canada and Jamaica agreed on terms to provide regular passenger and mail service between Halifax, Saint John, New Brunswick, Montreal, Quebec, and the West Indies. Canadian National Steamships received $10 million from the federal government to build the ships, which proved a popular distraction for the better off. Even at the height of the Depression, passengers still signed on for excursions to warmer climates.

During World War Two, the Lady Boats joined the Merchant Marine, were painted a dull grey in an attempt to avoid the attention of U-boats, and took part in many of the convoys that steamed across the Atlantic. Only two Lady Boats survived the war: *The Lady Nelson* and *The Lady Rodney*. *The Lady Rodney* is fondly remembered by hundreds of war brides.

But events like cruises to the Caribbean were for the rich—they had little effect on most of the immigrants passing through Pier 21. Few new immigrants remained in Halifax. Many were deported or, finding that work was scarce, returned to their countries of origin voluntarily. Others moved to Western Canada or the United States.

Nova Scotia's rural population was actually shrinking in the post-war years. Skilled farmers from Europe were encouraged to emigrate and the Canadian Department of Agriculture created the Land Settlement Branch.

In 1929 alone, 23 British and 15 Danish families settled on Nova Scotian farms. According to *A History of the Nova Scotia Farm Board*, the following year, 9 British and 21 Danish farming families immigrated.

In the late 1920s, skilled farmers were also required in other parts of the country, especially in Western Canada, as rural populations moved to the cities. But with the Great Depression, work in urban centres became hard to find and many families drifted back to the farms, in desperate need of financial help. Nova Scotia responded in 1932 with the Nova Scotia Farm Loan Board and the Miners Settlement Board. The idea was to use unemployed miners as farm labourers. Laudable though the scheme might have been, it met with limited success. As one new farmer wrote: "In the month of June 1932, my family and myself moved from Glace Bay to a farm, with the honest intention of making it my future home. We made every possible effort to make a living there but were unable to do so. I had about four acres of cleared land and, although I had all the stock and implements I could use on the place, I had to come back to the mines. I have always found the officers of the Board kind and courteous and willing to assist me in every possible way."

As economic conditions worsened, especially in Europe, more and more people expressed an interest in emigrating to Canada. This was particularly true in Denmark, where many young farmers could not afford to buy their own farms. In fact, in 1932, the Agricultural Attaché of the Netherland Legation in Washington made a trip to the province to determine what opportunities Nova Scotia had to offer immigrants.

By the 1930s, it was clear that Halifax needed an airport. Events in Europe, in particular the rise of militarism and the Nazi Party, hinted at trouble ahead. A few acres were cleared on land abutting Chebucto Road to create a runway for Royal Air Force training programs. Buildings were erected and facilities made available for Air Force personnel.

Despite concerns in Europe, immigration through Pier 21 continued at a slow pace. Immigration officer Fenton Crosman kept a diary of his dealings with new arrivals. He begins on December 17, 1936, writing: "I've been asked to report to Pier 21 in Halifax…all staff appear quite pleasant…scarcity of work here." The next day he appears to be a bit busier: "Have plenty of work today…Newfoundlanders applying for immigrant status in Canada…love this up-to-date Pier 21 and facilities."

continued on page 41

S.S. *Olympic* entering Halifax Harbour.

During the Depression years, although immigration nearly all but dried up, immigrant ships continued to arrive at Pier 21. Sometimes passengers arrived with high hopes only to find they could not make a living in Canada. They returned to their homelands back through Pier 21.

AERIAL VIEW NOVA SCOTIAN HOTEL and S.S. OLYMPIC, HALIFAX N.S.

COPYRIGHT. R. T. McCULLY

S.S. *Olympic* docked at Pier 21 with the Nova Scotian hotel in the foreground.

Other ships such as the S.S. *Britannic*, the White Star liner shown here at
Pier 21, sailed into Halifax, bringing immigrants. A total of 120 White Star
liners, including the infamous *Titanic*, operated from 1845 to 1936, at which
time White Star merged with Cunard.

Halifax has always welcomed cruise ships. In this photograph the RMS *Berengia* returns from a cruise to New York City on July 12, 1931.

In this idyllic photograph a couple on the Dartmouth side of the harbour watches ships come and go from Pier 21. It was the age of beautiful and well-appointed ships, especially for first-class passengers.

Five "Lady Boats," each named after the wife of a British naval admiral, were built in 1928. Intended as cargo ships to work the the trade between Canada's East Coast and the West Indies, they were also designed to take passengers in style on West Indian cruises, rather a clever way of augmenting income. Each ship had beautifully appointed reception and dining rooms and comfortable cabins. And the cost was reasonable: just $85 for a two-week holiday. The pre-war poster below shows *The Lady Rodney* emerging from behind swaying palms on a moonlit night.

In January 1937, Mr. Crosman, obviously more at ease with his job, writes, "have to interview a young immigrant Englishwoman, whose pregnancy has followed a little too closely on the heels of her marriage… parents have sent her to Halifax to protect her very respectable parents from shame." And on a sadder note, "Terrible tragedy today. A Polish immigrant child, only 5 years old, died in the Immigration Hospital and was buried today. She was accompanied by her parents, on their way to Western Canada. The Catholic Immigration Chaplain conducted the service in the Polish language."

On January 25, 1937, he reports jokingly, "The Cunard ship *Ascania* docked at the pier around 5:00 p.m.…have to work late tonite. An immigrant from Wales is intoxicated and very saucy…'You fellas can't keep me out of Canada!'" Yet the same month Mr. Crosman also reports, rather worryingly, "Also a German warship *Schlesien* is docked at Pier 21. Many people have come to see it." On May 6, 1937, the German airship *Hindenburg* flew along the coastline of Nova Scotia from Tidnish to Halifax, then along the south coast. With the *Hindenburg* hovering at just seven hundred feet above the ground, photographers on board took pictures of Nova Scotian ports, military installations and fortifications, and airplane factories in the Amherst area. It was evident that a European war with Germany was likely and that Canada, as part of the British Commonwealth, would be drawn into it.

Another sign of the coming war was a trickle of refugees from Europe who feared the advances of the Nazi Party in Germany. Of particular concern was the plight of European Jews. Since the early twentieth century, Jewish individuals and families have been emigrating to Canada, mostly from Eastern European countries where pogroms, officially sanctioned massacres of Jewish people, were not uncommon. For example, in 1923, approximately 3,500 Romanian Jews arrived at Pier 2 to be met by clerical organizations and members of the Halifax Jewish community. The Canadian Jewish community had pledged to the Canadian government that none of these newly arrived immigrants would become a public charge, a promise that was kept.

The rise of Nazism in the early 1930s worried the community, which tried desperately to convince the Canadian government to relax immigration laws to permit more Jewish people into the country. The Canadian National Committee on Refugees also joined the cause, but Jewish refugees and immigrants continued to be denied entrance to Canada. It fell to the Canadian Jewish Congress, organized "to co-ordinate, on a national basis, efforts to cope effectively and judiciously with internal and external problems," to campaign on their behalf.

In the 1920s, the congress was mostly concerned with the rights of Jewish people living in Canada, both Canadian citizens and landed immigrants. However, by the 1930s, the anti-Jewish bias of the Nazis, the increase in anti-Jewish articles in Canadian newspapers as the Depression bit deeper, and a racial riot in Toronto in August 1933 raised concerns among congress members. By 1938, the congress had established a refugee organization for Jewish people in an attempt to pressure the Canadian government to accept more refugees—to little avail.

That year, in an anguished letter to a Jewish family in Canada, a Jewish father living in Europe underscored the need for immediate government help: "In great distress and desperation, our family appeals to you for help. If no assistance comes, we shall all go under. Please help and save us. You are our last hope. We are very modest, have perfect manners and originate from a very old and esteemed family. If I cannot immigrate myself, I humbly beg that at least you can get my children a permit." This man's ominous words are reflected in an observation made by Fenton Crosman, who wrote in December 1938: "Department of Immigration imposes visa restrictions on all non-British Europeans…this new regulation is seen as stemming from the Jewish persecutions by the Nazis."

Just before World War Two, the Jewish World Congress made a desperate appeal to the Canadian government to allow displaced European children into Canada, promising that the congress would be responsible for their welfare. By 1942, congress leaders had pleaded with the government to alleviate the horrific conditions facing Jewish refugee children. Finally, on October 2, 1942, the Canadian government capitulated and gave permission for five hundred Jewish children from France, whose parents had been taken from them, to come to Canada—with the hope of an additional five hundred at a later date. In November 1942, before the rescue operation organized by France and Canada could be put into effect, the Nazis invaded France and the children were never heard of again.

But by that time Pier 21, already showing signs of wear after ten years of processing immigrants, had taken on another key role as troops amassed to join convoys headed to beleaguered Europe during World War Two. As an unidentified immigration officer wrote on March 10, 1937, two years before the outbreak of hostilities, "a gunboat arrives at the Pier …tonight Halifax is filled with officers, midshipmen and cadets."

Canada's 1st Division departs Pier 21 in December 1939. The division was made up of soldiers from all parts of Canada. The troops were equipped with battle uniforms of blouses, loose-fitting trousers, and gaiters. They took rifles and personal effects with them; other equipment was generally supplied once the soldiers arrived in England.

CHAPTER FOUR

Pier 21 during World War Two

Events in Europe overtook Pier 21. As the United Kingdom and its allies prepared to fight Nazi militarism in Germany and Italy, Canada—and Pier 21—were inexorably drawn in. It was, to paraphrase British Prime Minister Winston Churchill, the pier's "finest hour."

War was declared by Great Britain on September 3, 1939, after Germany invaded France. Canada swiftly followed suit, declaring war on its own behalf as an independent member of the British Commonwealth. But the country was ill prepared at first. Canada had little in the way of munitions industries, though that was soon to change. The Royal Canadian Navy consisted of six destroyers. In a matter of months, the navy grew in strength to 100,000 men and women, and its fleet included Canadian Merchant Marine ships, destroyers, corvettes, frigates, and minesweepers. The Air Force expanded to 250,000 men and women during the war years, while the Canadian Army had 730,000 soldiers in action. And at the centre of the movement of all these troops stood Pier 21, mobilized as an embarkation processing centre for those going overseas and debarkation centre for those returning, including the wounded.

At the start of the war, Halifax had a population of just 69,000. Those numbers quickly swelled to over 100,000 as workers poured into the city. The Halifax Shipyards were expanded and run night and day, even in winter sleet and ice, to repair and outfit 7,000 vessels. New tramlines were laid to ease city transportation and pre-fabricated houses sprang up to cope with an acute housing shortage.

Nova Scotia Light and Power, which had operated its first power station at the head of St. Margaret's Bay since 1919, responded quickly to a need for additional power. They erected a generator at Black River and a steam electric plant in Halifax. In addition to keeping the city's electrical supply safe and running, the company had to maintain radio-telephones, sirens, and generators. They also worked on mine detection equipment and developed sensitive mine equipment for the *Ramilles* and the *Emerald*, two of the ships that gave chase to Germany's *Bismarck*.

This was a city at war and on high alert. Blackout practices were frequent, gas masks were readily available, and patrols protected the coastline from German submarines as far as 85 kilometres out to sea. Despite a German attempt to ring the harbour with 56 mines on May 28, 1943, sweepers quickly cleared a path through.

Before the war, the Royal Canadian Navy had about 1,800 personnel and a handful of destroyers and minesweepers, and Halifax was not its main port. But as soon as war was declared, the city became the main base and training centre for naval personnel. One of its first acts in 1939 was to string a submarine defence net, made of steel cable, across the harbour entrance as a precaution against German U-boat attacks.

Pier 21 quickly shifted to a war footing. The building was put under the jurisdiction of Canada's Department of National Defence. The facility was chosen because it was large enough to handle the sheer numbers of military troops arriving and departing daily. About 500,000 service personnel left Canada through this rather plain building during the war years. Also Pier 21 abutted the Canadian National Railway (CNR) lines, which made it much easier to process soldiers arriving at the train station.

As Harry Walker of the 8th Canadian Hussars said, "CNR brought trainload after trainload of troops in. Pier 21 looked like a 'City of Soldiers.' As the ships sailed into Halifax Harbour and docked at Pier 21, we were designated to a particular ship." William Barker added: "When we arrived in Halifax we were parked on a siding waiting to be shunted to Pier 21. People came by the train to wish us good luck and brought along some 'cheers.' I remember the IODE members would give each of us a package filled with comfort items for our journey overseas…Pier 21 was a very nice place leaving from to go overseas, but a more enjoyable pier coming home." And so it must have been.

The first troops arrived at the pier by train in December 1939. They formed Canada's 1st Division, a contingent of around 7,500 men who left from Pier 21 aboard such ships as the *Aquitania, Empress of Britain, Duchess of Bedford, Monarch of Bermuda,* and the *Empress of Australia,* shepherded by four Canadian destroyers. Other troops soon followed as many of the world's most gracious liners were turned into troop carriers. One was the *Queen Elizabeth*; it and its sister ship, the *Queen Mary,* were the only two troop ships able to outrun German U-boats. About 14,000 soldiers sailed aboard the *Queen Elizabeth* on its maiden voyage as a troop ship.

The reality of war sank in with the loss of the *Athenia* on September 3, 1939. Filled with 1,300 troops and civilians, only 221 survived. Many were picked up by other ships and brought to Pier 21. One survivor, D.G.B. Stewart, recalled, "We did not have our clothes off from September 3 until the 13…on the latter date a bath was the most welcome one we ever had."

With few exceptions, all Canadian servicemen and women who fought overseas during World War Two departed from Halifax, Nova Scotia. For most, these final hours on the waterfront, waiting to board ship, were fraught with a sense of anxiety and excitement as they wondered whether or not they would survive to see Canada and their loved ones again. We all owe a great deal to these men and women, many of whom sacrificed their lives. The legacy of their bravery lives on in personal stories like that of Harry Walker, Trooper, 8th Hussars, Canada's oldest miliary regiment:

"I started my basic training in Saint John in 1943," stated Mr. Walker. *"From there we were sent to Cape Breton for Beach Patrol. Shortly after that, I joined the New Brunswick Rangers. We were then sent to Camp Borden to train in armoured vehicles.*

"After all this training, the troops travelled by train to Sussex where we were kept in holding for three weeks. Then we moved by train to Pier 21 in Halifax, Nova Scotia.

"My first impression of Pier 21 was 'What a huge warehouse!' Trainload after trainload of troops came in that day. Pier 21 looked like a City of Soldiers.

"As the ships sailed into Halifax Harbour and docked at Pier 21, we were designated to a particular ship. I sailed on the Letitia, a 12,000-ton Norwegian cargo ship. At this point in my military career, I was part of the Reinforcement Unit (Infantry).

"Our troop sailed back to Pier 21 on the Ile de France," Mr. Walker recalls, *"and what a welcoming, glorious sight there. Pier 21 was full of tables, which were all set for breakfast. There was*

continued on page 46

Harry Walker, 8th Canadian Hussars. Walker, with the rest of the Hussars, received basic training in Saint John, New Brunswick, before being shipped to Halifax by train in 1943. From Pier 21 he set sail for Scotland aboard the *Letitia*, a Norwegian cargo ship converted to troop carrier. From there the Hussars were sent to Italy, where they found their mascot, a filly they named Princess Louise. After standing by the regiment on V-E Day, the horse was brought home to Saint John aboard the *Leerdam* and put to pasture at the Beauregard Farm in Hampton, New Brunswick.

Convoys of merchant ships, corvettes, and frigates set sail for the North Atlantic. These journeys were fraught with danger as U-boats lurked not far beyond the entrance to Halifax Harbour.

eggs, juices of every kind, bacon, toast, etc.—all of which we didn't have on the Front. There were people in white cook jackets giving us generous amounts of food and we could have as much as we wanted as long as we ate every bite."

William Barker, another veteran, recalls leaving Pier 21 and his lasting impressions:

"I was born on September 15, 1920 in Cobalt, Ontario. After leaving school I went to work in gold mines of Kirkland Lake and Timmins. I joined the army in Timmins in the summer of 1942 and did basic training in Chatham, Ontario. I then did advanced training in Petawawa, Ontario.

"I left there on a troop train for Halifax and the last good food I was to have for the next four years. When we arrived in Halifax we were parked waiting to be shunted to the pier. People came by the train to wish us good luck and brought along some cheers such as Black Horse beer and bottles of rum-runners' top of the line rum. You could stick your finger in the bottle, pull it out, lick it and use tears for a chaser. We sure could have used some of that on the voyage to Scotland. We drank tea that was made in a 100-gallon vat, and I don't think the wool was removed from sheep before cooking. I could go on forever about conditions on board ship but you can guess the rest. One more little item: as soldiers do all of their training on their feet, calluses occur. Cockroaches on board had our feet cleaned up in two nights.

"Pier 21 was a very nice place going over seas but a more enjoyable pier coming back.

RMS *Queen Mary*, one of the two luxury liners (the other being RMS *Queen Elizabeth*) to be converted to troop carriers. Both ships were extremely fast and could outrun the treacherous U-boats, so they were the only ships that could cross the Atlantic Ocean without an escort.

S. Tanner Collection

Aerial view of RMS *Queen Mary* converted to a troop ship and docked at Pier 21, on August 20, 1943.

The S.S. *Mauretania* at anchor at Pier 2 during World War One was the sister ship of the S.S. *Aquitania* which was used as a troop ship during both World Wars.

The *Mauretania* docked at Pier 21 in front of the *Aquitania*. Both ships were converted from passenger ships to troop carriers. After the war, they continued to bring immigrants and returning soldiers to Canada.

The RCMP *St. Roch's* captain Henry (Hank) Larsen. He described the ship as "an ugly duckling."

Despite restrictions, the Department of Immigration continued to work during the war years, processing arrivals with or without proper documentation. Immigration slowed to a trickle and especially after the attack on Pearl Harbor, Asians in particular were subject to restrictions. Very few new immigrants arrived, but the department was involved with foreign nationals (such as French soldiers from occupied France), who came to Canada to help fight with allies, prisoners of war, and returning Canadian soldiers and merchant mariners (including the wounded). In the early years, they had the British Guest Children to look after and, beginning in 1944, they began to handle the processing of war brides and their children. Even Prime Minister Winston Churchill made a stop through Pier 21 in 1943 and again in 1944. Before he left, he remarked dryly of Pier 21 to the people of Halifax, "We know your city is something more than a shed on a wharf."

It was the immigration officer who had to handle the day-to-day operations of Pier 21's Immigration Department, despite the restrictions. Fenton Crosman, who remained at Pier 21 throughout most of the war years, records his frustration in a diary entry of March 1940: "… never get bored with work at Pier 21 now…have problems with Immigration Medical Service…we sent an inspector to Bedford Basin to check crews or examine passengers on ships waiting for convoys. The Medical Officer visits only ships flying the yellow quarantine flag, indicating someone on board is ill…a motley crowd in detention quarters at Pier 21. Black seamen waiting for a ship to take them back to the West Indies…also two British seamen discharged from the Navy, where they are accused of sabotage."

The immigration officer had to deal with bewildered and frightened refugees from war-torn Europe. On March 15, 1941, an unidentified officer writes: "…a tough day…had to handle a passenger ship filled with immigrants…always the usual anxieties and delays…the ship arrived with a convoy…some of the immigrants reported several ships in the convoy were sunk." And Fenton Crosman, a few months later on July 1, writes: "…survivors from the torpedoed S.S. *Mercier* brought into the pier…there were several seamen, a Polish Jew, his wife and two children. The Jewish man is quite ill and is now in hospital. They brought diamonds worth about $16,000 with them…seems we're the port for all stranded people…Greeks, Rumanians…"

Prisoners of war also kept the immigration officers hopping. One officer recorded in January 1941, "… more German prisoners arrive at Pier 21…they try to escape en route to internment camps…but at least one has gotten away and has crossed the border to the United States." And in June of the same year, Fenton Crosman wrote in his diary: "…two men escaped from detention last night; a shipload of immigrants arrived this afternoon with insufficient papers, and one of the stenos is off with a sprained ankle…but we did capture two men, one of them being Dutch…have been prosecuted and put in jail so they will be safe for a while."

Pier 21 enjoyed triumphs and disasters during the war years. For example, in 1942, the RCMP vessel *St. Roch* docked at Halifax's Pier 21 having navigated the Northwest Passage — only the second vessel ever to sail the northern route and the first to manage it from the Pacific to the Atlantic. This feat established Canada's sovereignty in the Arctic during the difficult war years and extended Canada's control over the vast northern territories.

The *St. Roch*, built in North Vancouver, British Columbia, was launched May 7, 1928. It was only 104 feet long with a 24-foot, nine-inch beam. Although built as a schooner, it was re-rigged as a ketch. It was a rugged little ship, designed to withstand the onslaught of ice floes.

For eleven years, the *St. Roch* patrolled Canada's Arctic until its retirement in 1948. To Captain Henry (Hank) Larsen, it was an "an ugly *continued on page 55*"

continued on page 55

RCMP *St. Roch* successfully navigated the Northwest Passage from west to east in 1942, thus establishing Canada's claim to the Arctic. It was only the second ship to sail through the passage and the first to take the Pacific-Atlantic route. The ship was built for the RCMP as a supply ship serving Arctic detachments. It was also used as a floating detachment during winter, with dog sled patrols being sent out from the ship.

Bleak picture of wartime Pier 21 in winter.

View of the railway terminal in Halifax's South End on February 5, 1941. During the war years, the terminal was exceptionally busy, bringing in not only troops but also goods to be shipped to Great Britain by convoy.

A light cruiser sets out to protect a convoy of troopships.

duckling" but was a darling on the water that handled the massive ice floes with ease. Captain Larsen recalled, "We were not far from Vancouver when we received our first baptism of water…bad weather … our heavily laden vessel was almost completely submerged, causing large volumes of water to pour down onto those who were trying to get some sleep…a hard thing to do when one is constantly on the verge of being tossed out of one's bunk with each roll of the ship…some of our boys had never been on a vessel or salt water, but to their everlasting credit, they soon found their sea-legs."

Two years after its retirement, the *St. Roch* returned to the seas briefly and was sent to Halifax via the Panama Canal, making it the first ship to circumnavigate North America.

Pier 21 endured its own disaster. In 1944, a fire broke out on the upper floor, where immigrants were processed. Although no one was injured at the time, the upper floor was ruined and vital papers and equipment were destroyed.

The Lady Nelson, one of the original five lady boats, was quickly put on war status and repainted in camouflage colours. She was sunk at anchor in the West Indies, salvaged and commissioned as a hospital ship.

And there were two near misses. Ever mindful of the Halifax Explosion of 1917, and with so many ships at anchor during World War Two, naval police patrolled the harbour, warning sailors of the dangers of fire from leaking oil and other scum on the water. On April 10, 1941, the nightmare came true as the *Trongate* flashed its lights through the dark to request assistance. There was a fire below decks and the ship carried TNT. The crew quickly abandoned ship and the decision was taken to sink the *Trongate* before it could cause an explosion. The *Chedabucto* shattered the quiet of the night by firing 25 rounds into the *Trongate* just below the water line. At 3:25 a.m., the *Trongate* listed to one side and slipped through the waves.

White crosses mark the graves of Canadian soldiers who died liberating Holland. Canadians and Dutch still honour their memories, and cemeteries, like this one, are well tended.

Troopship *Ile de France* docked at Pier 21, March 17, 1948. On board are soldiers returning from war.

The RMS *Queen Elizabeth* bringing troops back to Pier 21.

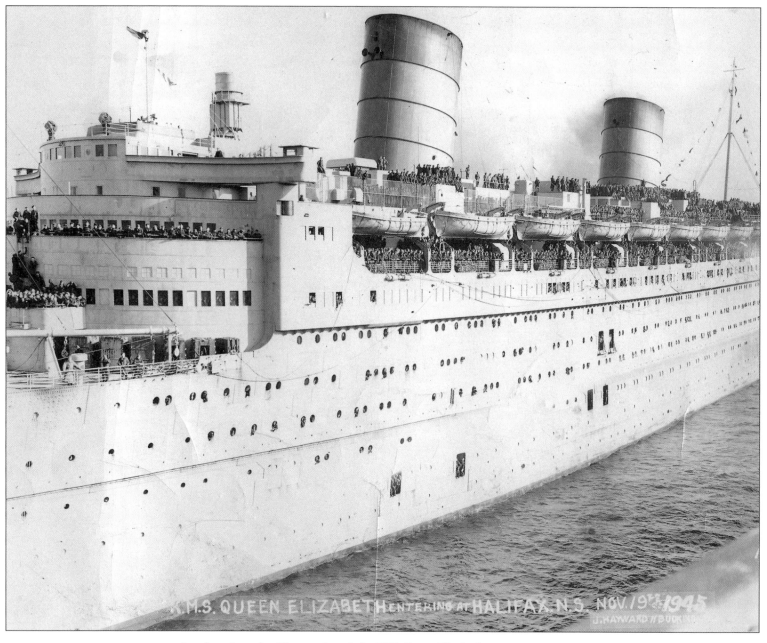

R.M.S. QUEEN ELIZABETH ENTERING AT HALIFAX. N.S NOV/9th/1945
J. HAYWARD // BUCKIN

Another view of soldiers on board the RMS *Queen Elizabeth*.

The hospital ship *El Nil* brings wounded soldiers back to Halifax. The wounded were met by medical personnel and quickly transferred to appropriate medical facilities.

The RMS *Queen Mary* bringing troops back to Pier 21.

One young woman reporting to work the next day got the fright of her life. As reported in the *Halifax Herald*: "…it became apparent that despite all the care taken in the *Trongate's* sinking, at least one shell had missed its mark, or perhaps went straight through the ship, and ricocheted ashore, where it crashed through the roof of a combination warehouse and office building, and came to rest inside. When one of the stenographers came to work this morning, the four-inch shell was sitting alongside her desk as neatly as if it had been placed there for exhibition" (Ron Inness). The second near disaster owed its aversion to valiant attempts by its crew to get help. The *Volunteer* was moored in the harbour. Senior staff, including the master, chief officer and chief engineer, quite inebriated, happily played cards on deck while below their feet the ship was on fire. The crew tried signalling for help but, unfamiliar with the port, used the wrong frequency and aimed their lights in the wrong direction. They couldn't jar a response from the senior officers and so abandoned ship, headed for shore, and summoned help. The fire department responded and tried to make the master understand the seriousness of the situation. Eventually he was persuaded to have the ship towed to McNab's Island and beached so that it would fill with water before it could explode.

Both these near misses could easily have destroyed Pier 21. Other wartime catastrophes had a lesser affect on the facility. On July 28, 1945, a munitions building on the Dartmouth side blew up. As smoke and fire filled the night sky, explosions continued, shaking buildings and breaking windows along Hollis and Barrington streets in downtown Halifax, and damaging and destroying some North End houses. As one witness, H.B. Jefferson, remarked, "Tonight lighting proved that it can strike twice in the same place or at least within a couple of miles of the same place." Another witness described the scene as looking: "like fireworks shooting into the air from the east side of Bedford Basin on the Dartmouth side. Then there was a ball of reddish flame and black smoke."

Pier 21 also managed to withstand two post-war riots. The first took place on the evening of May 7, 1945, after Victory in Europe or V-E Day, when a mob attacked and set a tramcar on fire. What started in a cheery, if inebriated, mood led to a seeming determination to take the downtown core of the city apart at its seams. Shop windows were smashed and looting was common. Victor Oland recalled an incident with his father: "During the riot my father got word that the rioters had broken into Keith's brewery so he went into the warehouse and he joined the brewery workers in giving each man a case of beer. When the men could see there was no more beer left, they disappeared without causing any damage."

Rioting occurred again on May 8. This time, as widespread vandalism and looting took place, the authorities decided to bring a thousand soldiers from Debert to quell the riot. Bars and liquor stores were closed and a curfew was set. Then the Admiral, accompanied by the mayor, drove through city streets with a loudspeaker, announcing: "Go to your billets, your ships, your quarters and your homes. This is an order. It is not a joke."

By 11 P.M., soldiers had cleared away the crowds and there was nothing left to do but mop up and make arrangements for reparations to those whose homes or buildings had been vandalized or looted.

Troops disembark at Pier 21, their homecoming marred somewhat by scenes of destruction following the Halifax riot.

Paper and broken glass litter the street as rioters flee during the V-E Day riots in Halifax. The riots began when a tramcar was set afire, and quickly escalated. The riot was most likely exacerbated by a decision to close bars and liquor outlets. Damages incurred in the few downtown blocks of Halifax amounted to hundreds of thousands of dollars and the city's reputation was besmirched.

Canadian merchant marines pose on board a ship at Pier 21. The sailor near the bottom may be evoking Prime Minister Winston Churchill's famous "V for Victory" sign. It was Churchill who paid tribute to the sailors by stating: "The Battle of the Atlantic was not won by our Navy or Air Force; it was won by the courage, fortitude and determination of allied merchant seamen."

CHAPTER FIVE

Canada's Merchant Marine

"The Battle of the Atlantic was not won by our Navy or Air Force; it was won by the courage, fortitude and determination of allied merchant seamen."
—Prime Minister Winston Churchill

"Their supreme sacrifice in both wars ensured the lifeline of men and of supplies without which victory could not have been ours and without which we would not now enjoy freedom.
—Book of Remembrance—The Merchant Navy

"Watched a convoy sail out of the Harbour in the misty sunlight…most of them oil tankers. Unlike the fancy camouflage used during the previous war, allied ships are painted either a dark grey from top to bottom, or with a black hull and a superstructure of brown or dirty yellow…one of the Cunard ships is now being used as an armed cruiser … it has its original coat of paint."
—Unidentified Immigration Officer at Pier 21, January 1940.

Most Canadians do not understand how the Canadian Merchant Navy operated during the war. Their service was "top secret." No reference was made to the ships' names, nor to their captains, cargo, tonnage, ports of departure, destinations, times of sailing and arrival. Through the years, members of the Canadian Merchant Navy have been criticized and false information about their efforts abounds. Only in recent years is the truth coming out. After the war ended, Merchant Navy mariners were excluded from all veterans' benefits. They paid a high price indeed for our country's freedom.

It wasn't until 1992 that the Canadian government finally granted the Merchant Navy veterans status under the Merchant Navy Veterans and Civilian War-Related Benefits. In December 1999, the government granted merchant mariners retroactive benefits.

When Canada declared war in September 1939, it had only 38 ocean-going merchant ships with approximately 1,450 Canadian seamen. Those that tried to enrol but were not taken included boys (between the ages of 14 and 16), older men (some were in their 70s), and physically challenged men (some had polio; others had poor eyesight).

During the war, the German Navy's intention was to control the oceans and to make sure supplies did not reach Great Britain and Europe, thereby hopefully forcing the Allies to surrender. The Germans built up their U-boat fleet quickly; it was, Winston Churchill said, "The only thing that ever really frightened me during the war…"

The Atlantic convoy of merchant marine ships became the lifeline of the war effort.

Between September 1939 and May 1945, approximately 25,343 merchant ships with 164,783,921 tons of cargo on board sailed from North America to Britain. Conditions must have been harrowing. Immigration officer

continued on page 70

A group of merchant seamen at dockside check the warmth of the sheep fleece lining of a vest. Keeping warm while at sea became a major occupation of sailors, especially in winter. Volunteer groups in Halifax such as the Imperial Order Daughters of the Empire did their best to provide sailors with warm clothing. They even unstitched ladies' leather gloves and refashioned them as vests for the merchant marines.

Stevedores busily unload TNT from a merchant ship.

Ships amass in Bedford Basin.

Once outside the harbour approaches, the ships begin to assume formation for the convoy. Here a gun ship signals individual ships to take their positions. Convoys travelled in tight formation, with corvettes protecting vulnerable ships and stragglers. Ships that broke down often had to be abandoned. The lot of the merchant marines was especially hazardous. The ships on which they sailed, filled with food, fuel, and supplies for Great Britain, were often placed on the outer edges of the convoys. Troop ships occupied the better-protected areas in the centre.

Fenton Crosman recorded in his diary that desertion among seamen was a very real problem: "I'm trying to cope with seamen deserting from freighters…passengers ships are few and far between…Halifax is on a war footing…censorship of the mails…many freight ships either dock at Pier 21 or wait in the basin for a convoy…can't keep up with deserting seamen. I have been told to start boarding ships to check for enemy aliens, stow-aways and the Chinese." (January 1940).

One unidentified immigration officer at Pier 21 remarked in October 1940: "merchant seamen don't want to sail again once they arrive at the Pier…the merchant navy is the most important during wartime…one can hardly blame these men for their reluctance to return to sea…the ships are old, they work under appalling conditions, and they are sitting ducks for the numerous enemy submarines."

The Battle of the Atlantic was the longest battle of the war and the Merchant Navy was committed to it from day one. It was a crucial task to ensure that the sea-lanes were open and that cargo essential to the war effort reached its destination, regardless of the U-boat peril and lack of protection, even from the air. These ships carried troops, weapons, equipment, fuel, and supplies such as mail, steel, lumber, and foodstuffs.

Elblic Koblouski, a Canadian merchant marine, wrote: "One of the ships carried thousands of tons of ammunition. One of the regulations aboard this ship was that sailors must wear life jackets at all times. At one point, the captain of the ship noticed that I was not wearing my life jacket. The captain, of course, demanded to know why. I replied, 'There's so much ammunition on board and if we get a direct hit, I don't need a life jacket; I need a parachute to come down'."

The Canadian merchant marine ships were ill equipped and took great risks while serving their country. "The North Atlantic was a terrible-looking place in 1942…it looked like a graveyard," remarked Canadian merchant marine Paul Brick. When a convoy was attacked by U-boats, there were two options: maintain formation and fight as best as they could or split the formation and try to outrun the enemy separately. Merchant ships were the "sitting ducks" and it must have been mental torture watching their own ships being torpedoed and thinking of their lost comrades.

By 1943, the Allies had control of the seas. The Battle of the Atlantic had been won with the efforts and sacrifices of those who sailed in merchant marine ships. Canada lost approximately 1,200 merchant seamen as a result of enemy action—one in ten—higher than any of the branches of the Canadian armed services. George Evans' story typifies the courage of the merchant marines:

"The Battle of the Atlantic was one of the most crucial battles in the Second World War. This battle continued day in and day out from 1939 until 1945…men faced enemy guns above the sea; bombs of enemy aircraft; torpedoes from German U-Boats; moving through floating mine fields…German U-boats sank 75 Canadian merchant ships, 24 Canadian warships."

As a young boy, George Evans never tired of watching the various ships come and go in the harbour at St. John's, Newfoundland. By the time World War Two had started, the town was extremely busy. Army and navy barracks were being built. Sirens went off unexpectedly. Ships in the harbour were camouflaged. Vehicles were driven with dimmed headlights. St. John's was a town under war conditions.

Young George yearned to enlist, but at age 15, he was told he was too young. Undaunted, he boarded the 2000-ton Norwegian cargo ship, S.S. *Einvik*, while it lay in the harbour. The crew consisted of Norwegians, and Canadians but just one Newfoundlander—George Evans. He cleared the mess deck, scrubbed pots and pans, did galley duty, made bunks, and cleaned the officers' quarters. He was a hard worker and his efforts impressed the skipper. All the same, George had to find ways to avoid his captain, who repeatedly asked him for his birth certificate.

In the first week of September 1941, the S.S. *Einvik* set sail from St. John's with a convoy of destroyers and corvettes. George Evans was somewhere aboard. The ship tried hard to keep up with the rest of the convoy but it was slow. The engine broke down. The waves towered. And it was dark: no lights could be used in case the enemy U-boats were attracted by them. George recalled, "I was sick, scared and afraid, miles from no where tossing on the Atlantic like a cork…."

One night, to his horror, he was awoken in his bunk by a tremendous explosion "I grabbed my lifejacket and ran out for the lifeboat deck…on the way I heard that a torpedo had struck us. Then shells kept hitting the ship and it was on fire."

George was helped into a lifeboat but not what he considered to be the right one—the captain was in that lifeboat too! For nine days, the eleven members of the crew on that lifeboat floundered in the cold Atlantic. Sometimes they would row. If a breeze came up, they hoisted the sail.

There was a little bread and some drinking water, but the crew were in bad shape. All George wanted to do was lie down and sleep. After a gruelling time, the crew were rescued by some Icelandic fishermen who warmed them with food, hot chocolate, and tea, and took them to Iceland's Westmann Island, where they were hospitalized.

Two weeks later George Evans boarded a ship to Scotland where he joined the S.S. *Daytonian* as a fireman/trimmer. Next he was posted to the Dutch ship S.S. *Aurora*, taking cargo to Belfast, Ireland, and various ports in the English Channel. After that it was the S.S. *Pieter De Hoogh*, which sailed to North Russia and made a number of runs to American ports, South America, then back to Russia. The Russian runs were gruelling—icy cold spray and snow coated the ship's decks and the crew often neared starvation as they awaited supplies. It must have been a relief for George to find himself aboard the British ship S.S. *Fort Charnisay*, which sailed to Mediterranean ports. In 1945, George Evans was at last posted on the S.S. *Dorelain*, which sailed from England to Pier 21. Shortly after arriving in Halifax, he returned to his home and family in Newfoundland.

Graham Gates, now in his 90s, was a member of the merchant marine from 1936 to 1947. when war was declared, he and his mate tried to join the Canadian Navy, only to be laughed at by the recruiting officer. "Why would you want to join the Navy?" he was asked. "The only place you're wanted," the officer continued, "is right where you are—in the merchant marines."

"Mum" was the watchword. So secretive were the movements of Canada's merchant marine during World War Two that the names of captains and crews were often unknown. German U-boats menaced convoys crossing the Atlantic, so it was essential that information regarding the sailing times and destinations of ships not fall into enemy hands.

THE MERCHANT SERVICE IS *Silent* TOO !

DON'T TALK ABOUT CARGOES OR SHIP SAILINGS

The late Doug Dauphinee, friend of Graham Gates and crew member aboard the oil tanker MV *Regina Lite*.

Gun on the deck of the *SS Colborne*. Naval personnel were usually assigned to merchant marine ships to handle the guns. But the S.S. *Colborne*, stationed in the Pacific Ocean, broke down and the crew spent two months near Cape Town, South Africa. During his enforced stay on land, Graham Gates took a course to learn how to handle the gun himself.

MV (Motor Vessel) *Regina Lite* in rough seas. Graham Gates was one of very few sailors who had a camera on board. Cameras were forbidden, except in the hands of official Navy or Air Force photographers, in case film fell into enemy hands.

Graham Gates and his grandson peer over the memorial to the veterans of the Canadian Marine Navy.

Not all sailors were lucky enough to make it to a lifeboat. Here marines tread water while awaiting rescue. About half of the crews of merchant marine ship sinkings did not survive.

The Lady Drake, one of the five elegant Lady Boats that plied the waters between Halifax and the West Indies in the 1930s, was an unfortunate casualty of the Battle of the Atlantic. Pressed into war service and abandoned by a convoy that had been ordered to detour to Guantanamo, *The Lady Drake* set out alone from Bermuda on May 3, 1942. Despite evasive moves to prevent a U-boat attack, at 9 P.M. on May 8, a torpedo rammed into the number three hold, shattering it. Within 20 minutes, 265 passengers and crew had taken to the five lifeboats. Twelve people in the vicinity of the hold at the time of the explosion died. Survivors found themselves alone in the ocean and feared a return of the U-boat. Then the lifeboats were passed by the swift *Queen Mary* enroute to New York City. There was no question of the *Queen Mary* stopping to pick up the survivors: that would have compromised the ship. But the *Queen Mary's* crew flashed a signal that lifeboat positions would be reported on arrival in New York. It was still several days before an American patrol plane finally spotted the lifeboats and directed the USN *Owl* to the rescue.

Ships of Acadia Overseas Freighters Limited at the Halifax dockyard in February or March 1950.

British guest children arriving in Halifax in 1941. Each child was issued a small suitcase and given a list of clothing and toys that could be taken with them. They travelled not only to Canada but also to other parts of the Commonwealth, including Australia, New Zealand, and South Africa. In all, about 3000 children were sent to Canada during the early war years.

CHAPTER SIX

Hosting British Guest Children

"For me, Pier 21 was indeed an entrance into a new world."
—a British evacuee child

By 1940, the war in Europe was going badly for the Allies. British cities and military installations were under constant bombing by the Luftwaffe who, under Hitler's direction, had turned to targeting civilians. Fearing a Nazi invasion, many English families decided to send their children to safety in one of the British dominions: Canada, Australia, New Zealand and South Africa. The Children's Overseas Reception Board (CORB) was established and families were given an opportunity to apply to have their children placed with a foster family for the duration of the war. After it was over, the children were to be returned. Most families felt that it would be a matter of months rather than years.

In all, about seven thousand British evacuee children or "British guest children," as they became known, made the trip to Canada between 1939 and 1940, with three thousand passing through Pier 21. For many of these children, taken suddenly from their families and sent off into an unknown future, it must have been terrifying. Immigration Officer Fenton Crosman recorded the arrival of some of the first in 1939, "We are all very busy but try to welcome and handle each and every person as best we can. The British Evacuee Children are starting to arrive…some of the immigration (workers) and guards give pennies to the children…they are eagerly received and cherished by the young arrivals. They tell us that the most unusual thing they notice on arrival in Halifax is the absence of blackouts at night. England has been shrouded in darkness for so many months."

A year or so later, London's *Sunday Chronicle*, dated September 8, 1940, included a column that read: "More Children Reach Canada. More children sent by the Children's Overseas Reception Board have arrived safely at Pier 21 in Halifax, Canada—no doubt to the relief of their parents." On August 26, 1940, Fenton Crosman added in his diary, "The Government-sponsored scheme for the evacuation to Canada of British children is working…we now have more ships for convoy duty…now a fleet of ships has arrived at the Pier, carrying approximately fourteen hundred youngsters for placement in homes throughout Canada for the duration of the war. I imagine it will be difficult for the children and their temporary foster parents to get used to each other." Mr. Crosman's intuition led him to conclude, "I think some of these children will remain in Canada."

On September 17, 1940, disaster struck. The *City of Benares*, carrying about ninety children, was sunk by a U-boat torpedo. Here seventy-seven of the children and their adult escorts lost their lives. After that disaster, it was considered too dangerous to try to remove the children at the height of the Battle of the Atlantic. Fenton Crosman recorded the tragedy, "The evacuation of British children is being put on hold…a terrible tragedy at sea on September 17, 1940—the British *City of Benares* was sunk by an enemy submarine, with 250 souls perishing…77 were evacuee children…50 survived and were found and brought to Halifax."

Not all children were welcomed with the same enthusiasm. Very few British children of Jewish descent were received, according to Geoffrey

Bilson who was recorded by Michel Fethney in *The Absurd and The Brave* as saying: "The Children's Overseas Reception Board sent twelve Jewish children among the 1,148 evacuees in the first four parties to Canada." He also added that: "'Coloured children' were excluded from the scheme at the request of host countries."

Those who made the trip were welcomed at Pier 21 and handed on safely to their host families. Although parents had hoped to see their children by Christmas 1940, many of these young people stayed for four or more years with their host families. Some lost their natural parents during the blitz and never returned. Others went back home after the war and found it difficult to readjust to family they hadn't seen in years and under strict post-war rationing. A number elected to return to Canada as adult immigrants. Fenton Crosman had been right.

The stories told by adults who arrived in Canada as children seeking safety convey both the problems of the evacuation scheme and its merits.

"Being a member of the first group of British children evacuated to Canada under the terms of the Children's Overseas Reception Board (CORB) scheme, was a great privilege. It was to prove one of the most wonderful and beneficial events of my life.

"Following a miserable seasick passage, and despite two attacks by enemy submarines, entry through Pier 21 allowed me to escape the horrors of war and to experience the safety, the beauty, the vastness of Canada, and later, the generous rewards of becoming a Canadian citizen.

"Like many other children brought to this country during stressful times, I was welcomed into the homes and the lives of a young, loving and extremely generous couple who cared for my every need during the war years. During my formative years, they nurtured and guided me as one of their own; when the need arose, they comforted and consoled me; and they contributed immeasurably to my welfare and my education through their guidance and financial aid.

"I had what was probably an unusual experience when I entered Canada through Pier 21 in August of 1940. I was coming as an evacuee from Scotland going to stay with distant relatives in Kingston, Ontario. I was seven years old and was sent over, on the Duchess of York *I think, with a friend of a friend of my parents who was coming to Canada to get married in Toronto. She put me out of the train in Kingston when it stopped for a few minutes, but that was after our experience in Halifax.*

"After we disembarked at Halifax she had a problem convincing the immigration officer that she was who she said she was, and his suspicions were confirmed when he addressed her in Gaelic and she could not reply to him. Apparently he was from Cape Breton and could not accept that someone from Scotland did not have the language used in the Garden of Eden. She was locked up overnight and I was put in the care of the Red Cross until the next day when she was able to get to her baggage and establish her identity! We were then put on a train to Kingston. That was my introduction to Canada!" (Alan Cairnie).

Although Catherine MacKinnon Read and her sister Anne never quite made it to Pier 21, as their ship was diverted to Quebec City, their story typifies what so many guest children to Canada experienced.

"When France capitulated in June 1940, the threat of invasion of Britain by Germany appeared to be imminent as France became an excellent base for the Germans.

"I vividly remember being awakened, and running to our neighbour's air-raid shelter in Falkirk, Scotland, as German planes flew overhead. They repeatedly tried to bomb the Forth Bridge nearby, as it was used for the transportation of vital armaments and supplies.

"In July, I heard about the C.O.R.B. for the first time. However, evacuation was never discussed in our family. In August, therefore, I was totally surprised—and shocked—when my mother told my sister Anne and, later, me that we were leaving for Canada within forty-eight hours with other Scottish evacuees. At that time, everyone expected that the war in Europe would be over within a year. There was no time to analyse the situation, or consider the risk involved.

"The following morning, Anne and I, each carrying an eighteen by twenty-six inch case, a knapsack and a gas mask, said good-bye to our parents and left by taxi. My favourite teacher, Margaret Chalmers, accompanied us to the railway station—and that was reassuring! My reaction to being evacuated was typical of an eleven year-old child who adored the American movie star, Shirley Temple, and dreamed of someday learning to sing and speak with an American accent. This was very exciting, as I had not faced the reality of the situation of not knowing where we were going or how long we were going to be away from home.

"We travelled to Glasgow by train where we were billeted in a large school. We were delayed, for security reasons, before going to Gourock. On August 16th,

British guest children on deck of an unidentified ship, docked at Pier 21 (1940). These children were sent by their parents to Canada to be safe from bombing by the Luftwaffe or the possibility of invasion by the Germans. In 1940, many Britons thought the war would be over in a matter of months and their children would be returned to them by Christmas. In fact, most of the evacuees stayed until 1945 or 1946, and some of the older children adapted so well to Canada that they never returned. While these children look excited, for many young people it was a terrifying journey. They left behind homes and families, unsure if they would ever see them again, and sailed into the unknown. There was every chance their ship might be torpedoed. While they were met at Pier 21 by friendly volunteers who placed them with foster families, it must still have been a daunting experience for such young children.

we sailed down the Firth of Clyde on the S.S. Bayano. My sister recorded that she was optimistic and happy, as she regarded this as an adventure. However, as I stood on deck watching the gigantic waves, I became aware of the vast distance separating our family, as well as the danger of being at sea during wartime. Standing beside me, there were five members of one family—the Baines—and I remember how concerned I was for their parents. I noticed, too, that some of the crew on the Bayano appeared to be not much older than some of the evacuees. Those boys, as well as our escorts, went out of their way to keep us happy by organizing games and concerts. The most memorable event, for me, was the wonderful birthday party given for those of us whose birthdays were in August. As there were ninety-nine children, the cake was the largest I had ever seen; it was spectacular!

"The following day, we spotted an iceberg, and later, we sighted land. However, we could not sail into Halifax, and Pier 21, as planned because of the presence of many German U-Boats. On August 27th, we sailed up the St. Lawrence River to Quebec City where the bright lights were in sharp contrast to the blackouts in Scotland!

"On August 28th, we sailed on to Montreal where we were given a very warm reception. I recall being amazed when a Red Cross lady handed me a chocolate bar, through the window of the train, and would not accept any payment. When she gave me a second treat, I thought that I was in the "land of milk and honey."

"Travelling on the night train to Toronto was a great experience. We stayed at Hart House, University of Toronto, for two weeks until full medical procedures were completed. Red Cross, as well as Children's Aid Workers, interviewed us to gain information so that we could be placed in appropriate homes. It was great having no food rationing, and soap and shampoo were plentiful. Sleeping on mattresses on the gym floor was rather like camping.

"On September 6th, we boarded a train for Ottawa, and were billeted temporarily in three different homes. Although I was profoundly homesick, I shall never forget the kindness and sensitivity of these Canadian families. Finally, Anne and I were placed in the same home—we were very fortunate. Like most hosts, the Malcolms had volunteered to take in pre-teen evacuees—but they unselfishly accepted us—not knowing how long we would be in Canada. Their daughter, Phyllis, in Grade 13, made us feel entirely welcome, and their son Andy, a Grade 9 student, introduced me to the neighbourhood gang. Although I was rather young for High School, I was warmly accepted. Being in Glebe Collegiate's choir, learning to ski and to skate on the Rideau Canal, Ottawa, and

C.G.I.T. Camp were great experiences. Everyone was very supportive and this helped me with adjusting to the new environment.

"Other evacuees were not so fortunate. The City of Benares was torpedoed in September 1940 and 77 of the 90 evacuees were lost, as well as 6 of the 10 escorts.

"Anne returned to Scotland in 1944—and I left Canada in 1945. I remember standing on board the ship and hearing news vendors call out: 'Les Japonais ont capitule!'

"In Edinburgh, my parents were very supportive of my studying there for three years to become a teacher. In 1948, they were exceptionally understanding when I could not decide on which side of the Atlantic to settle. They encouraged me to return to Ottawa and try teaching for a year before making the decision. However, there is a happy ending! A major event influenced my decision. When I went to board the S.S. Ascania in Liverpool, I met a Dalhousie University student returning from Europe. Three years later, in 1951, we were married in Halifax. My parents later emigrated to Canada. Now, 49 years later, Gordon and I have retired in Nova Scotia, and have been proud to have our children and grandchildren visit Pier 21.

"In retrospect, I realize that my parents were exceptional people to let us go during the vital years of our development. My host family was remarkable to share their lives with total strangers. They, and the Red Cross and Children's Aid Workers, in Scotland and Canada, as well as the crew of the S.S. Bayano, have profoundly enhanced and influenced my life. I truly love, and appreciate, each one of them" (Catherine MacKinnon Read).

In September 2001, child evacuees sent from Pier 21 to families on Prince Edward Island held a 61st anniversary reunion in Charlottetown. Holding hands and singing "Auld Lang Syne" are: Frank Roberts, Mary (Roberts) Mayger, Audrey (Pitt) Leavens, Stella (Pickering) Bates, Malcolm Joyce, Peter Raven, and Muriel Pitt.

A group of war brides and their children docked at Pier 21.

CHAPTER SEVEN

War Brides

1944: "…ship has arrived with over two thousand service-men and officers and over 100 civilians, some being war brides with their children…one lost her six-month old baby during the voyage. The child was smothered when a coat hanging above the berth fell on it while it was asleep…one little one keeps running around and around and says, 'Mummy, I don't see any people around here with blue noses.' Needed a chuckle!"
—Fenton Crosman, Immigration Officer

With hundreds of thousands of Canadian troops stationed in Europe during and after the war, it was inevitable that many of these soldiers would marry European women and arrange for them and their children to emigrate to Canada. About 50,000 war brides and 22,000 children arrived at Pier 21 towards the end of the war or in the years immediately following. They came from the United Kingdom, France, Holland, Belgium, Ireland, Italy, and Newfoundland (then still a British colony) aboard ocean liners such as *Aquitania*, *Mauretania*, *Queen Elizabeth*, *Queen Mary*, *Lady Rodney*, *Ile de France,* and *Pasteur*.

These brave and adventurous women left everything familiar behind and came to cities and rural areas across Canada, often ill prepared for the conditions they were to find. Though some later returned to their homelands, most adapted to and grew to love Canada, displaying a pioneering spirit and resilience.

Many of the war brides were married overseas but some waited until they had arrived in Canada to marry their Canadian fiancés. Those who married in Canadian towns often didn't have a wedding dress. The devastation in Europe after the war made luxury items like wedding dresses nearly impossible to obtain. And so the Imperial Order Daughters of the Empire (IODE) in Halifax/Dartmouth arranged for boxes of wedding dresses to be shipped overseas.

All the brides were met at Pier 21 when they arrived in Halifax. Those who arrived in daytime might have been met by volunteers from such organizations as the IODE, the Red Cross, or the Young Women's Christian Association (YWCA). Volunteers answered war brides' questions, helped care for their children, made sure they had the right documentation, even put them aboard trains taking them to their new homes. If their ship arrived at night, it might have been just their husbands and an immigration officer present to greet them. All war brides had their own stories. Here are just a few:

Ada Elizabeth Mills was born in Woolwich, England. Her family moved to Reigate, England, when Ada was eleven years old. At the time World War Two was declared in 1939, Ada, like most young women, worked in a factory.

In Canada, George Langley was with the Black Watch Miliary Reserve in Montreal and was called into service in 1939. He left Montreal for Halifax via train and departed from Pier 21, where he boarded one of the many troopships leaving for Britain.

George and Ada met in Reigate, England, in a pub. After courting for a time, George and Ada married in April 1942. Their reception was held in Reigate, with Ada's family and friends and George's fellow servicemen in attendance.

The Lady Rodney brought thousands of war brides to Canada—so many, in
fact, that one group of immigrants wrote an ode to the ship.

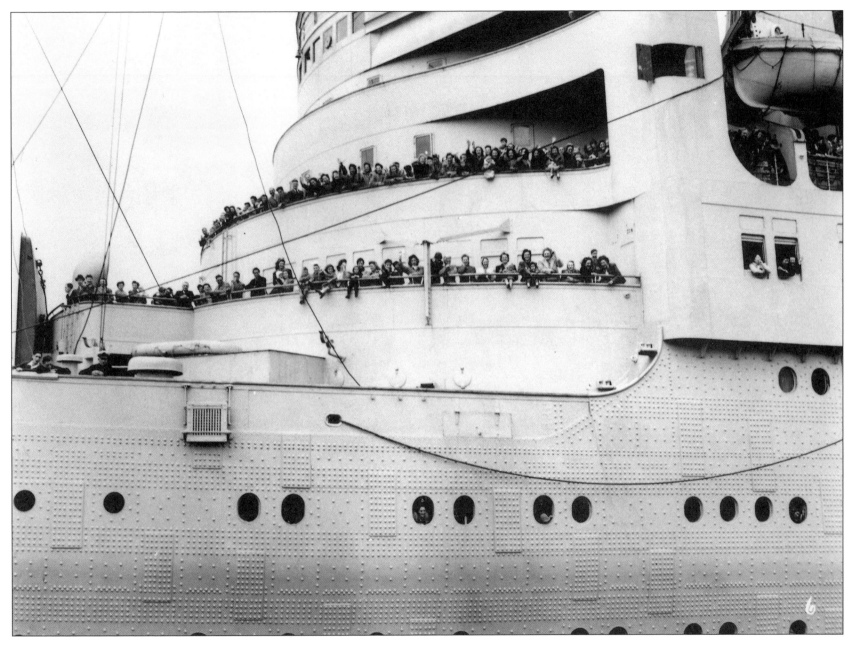

RMS *Queen Elizabeth*, May 27, 1946.

R.M.S. "MAURETANIA" ARRIVING AT HALIFAX, N.S. AUG 24th 1946 WITH WAR BRIDES etc.
THE LORD ARCHBISHOP of CANTERBURY & FIELD MARSHAL VISCOUNT MONTGOMERY C.B. D.S.O.
J. HAYWARD 11 BUCKINGHAM ST HALIFAX N.S.

RMS *Mauretania*, August 24, 1946.

In September 1944, George and Ada had their first child, James William. George served in Holland and was part of the D-Day operations. After the war, George returned home to Montreal. Ada and infant James left in June 1945 for Liverpool, where they joined other war brides and their children on the Volendam, which travelled to Pier 21. Ada recalls, "aboard ship there were nurses who cared for the children so the war brides could deal with luggage and paper-work." The trip from England to Canada across rough seas took about five days. Upon their arrival, nurses looked after James so that Ada could go through the immigration process. She recalls, "people helped the war brides right to the point where they boarded the trains. On the jour-ney, I couldn't believe that all the homes were made of wood." Ada felt fortunate that when they arrived in Montreal, she and James were met by family mem-bers. Ada, like many war brides, had to adjust to her new life in Canada—not everything was a "rose garden."

After six months, George and Ada received wartime hous-ing, but work was difficult to find in Montreal because so many servicemen were being discharged from the army. George and Ada decided to move back to England in September 1946. They went through Pier 21 again not only with James but also with their daughter, Carol. They crossed the Atlantic aboard the Ascania, and settled in Reigate. The family was very happy. Two more children, Margaret and Catherine, were born in England. George was an only child and his parents in Montreal asked and hoped that he and his family would consider moving back to Montreal. In September 1955, George and Ada did return, again aboard the Ascania. Today, Ada lives in Nova Scotia.

Postcard to an American friend by a woman staying in Halifax and watching various ships carrying war brides arrive at Pier 21.

Eileen Black—*"In September 1940, our home was demolished by a parachute bomb and my mother died in January 1942 as a result of her injuries. I was buried and then rescued by my father, but luckily I was not injured.*

"I married a Canadian soldier in November of 1941 and looked forward to the time when I would be coming to Canada. The time finally came in July 1946 and by then I had two children ages four and two. My husband had been home a full year so we were very anxious to follow him. When I was due to leave, my father came to London to say goodbye. It was with mixed feel-ings that I left but nevertheless, I was excited to be on my way at last.

"The voyage over was a little difficult, looking after the two chil-dren and trying not to be seasick. When we arrived in Halifax, I remember that it was very hot and as we only had to go as far as Montreal, we were some of the last ones to go ashore. Finally we board-ed the train and settled in for a night's sleep. The train was late and didn't arrive until late at night. By that time everyone was very tired. My husband and his family were at the station to meet us; we were finally together again.

"We lived in Montreal for the next two years and I was lucky that several other war brides from my hometown had also married men from Montreal. In 1957, we decided to venture out west. By then we had two more children. We sold everything and bought a station wagon and camped our way across the country taking twenty-six days. Finally we arrived in Vancouver with no job, no furniture and very little money. The first years in Vancouver were very difficult but we managed and never regretted moving. We are now retired and have seven grandchildren. Thank goodness we are both healthy and enjoy life.

"In 1989, I became a member of the Vancouver War Brides Association. I have never been sorry that I came to Canada."

Marriage of Mini Porter and Allan Porter. Many Canadian soldiers involved in the liberation of The Netherlands fell in love with and married Dutch women.

Dorothy Powell arrived aboard *The Lady Rodney* on May 24, 1946. She and her Canadian husband, Ron, married in England in July of the previous year. When asked how she enjoyed Canada, she replied that she'd reserve judgement until she'd been in the country for four seasons. "Needless to say, I stayed," she concluded.

Cover of a pamphlet designed to help war brides adjust to their lives in Canada. Chapters include information on what Canadians like to eat, how they dress, who they are, and what each province is like.

Hilda Bradshaw—*"Our journey to Canada started in Southampton on the Aquitania, July 22, 1946. I remember the good food on board ship, and although I was so seasick, I especially remember the 'white dinner rolls.' Although I couldn't eat, I took a white dinner roll back to the cabin with me to show the girls who couldn't make it to the dining room, so we could all gaze at it in wonder. We hadn't seen bread so white for a very long time. On reaching Nova Scotia and Halifax's Pier 21 we got all our things sorted out alphabetically, on the train we went. Being shown to our seats, we were thrilled to find we had a whole seat each, but found we needed the extra space, as the journey to Saskatchewan was a long one. It was interesting to see the various provinces roll by. A lot of us had not travelled too far from home during the war, what with the London Blitz, etc.*

"I was lucky, having been brought up in a military school in the Nilgiri Hills in S.W. India, because my father had been in the British Army in India before she got her independence in 1947. This would also have been the first time a number of the 'war brides' as we were named, had been parted from their families, which was hard for them. We looked forward to seeing our husbands again with a mixture of excitement and apprehension, but we were determined to make the best of things, so we put on a smile and took our first steps into a land, which we knew nothing about. Things were, of course, very different, and we slowly got used to Canadian ways.

"I went on to Saskatoon, Saskatchewan, and was tickled to see a city so clean after grimy London. I was disappointed to find out that we were not going to live in Saskatoon but that I had another train journey to Carrot River, of all places. This was news to me; we arrived in Carrot River in darkness and my husband and I were met by my father-in-law and an older English couple who had a car. We drove out to the farm we were going to live on (another surprise) along a dirt road, which was very narrow and there was thick brush on either side. Imagine my thoughts, surrounded by complete strangers, except my husband. I hoped that another car was not coming from the other direction. London has narrow streets, but this was quite nerve-racking. My father-in-law was a very sweet person, but he had said 'Let's get her home tonight before day break because if she sees Carrot River in the daylight she will go back right away.' We laughed about that, years later. However, I did stay and learned to do everything a farm wife was supposed to do: canning, bread making, making pies, cakes, butter and all the rest of it. I learned a lot and people were so helpful.

"We were always treated so well on our journey, and my thanks goes out to all, from on board ship to Pier 21, and on the train. We were well received on the whole, but unfortunately there were some girls who were not well received by some Canadian families, sad to say."

Janet Prentice—*"My husband Cpl. James Reid Paton arrived two days ahead of me on the Ile de France, a troop ship. I sailed from Liverpool. The day after I got on the train to go to the ship the railroad went on strike in Scotland. They took us to military barracks for about three days before we left. It was mayhem with crying children, parents of the war brides crying, disorganization everywhere.*

"I volunteered to be an escort for a little boy named Johnie, age three. He was coming to Canada to be with his father who was a Canadian soldier in the European campaign. His mother had abandoned him. It was a traumatic crossing because I was a stranger to Johnie. The Red Cross nurses were very helpful during the crossing. On board our ship there were 32 soldiers who had volunteered to fight in Japan. Fortunately for them the Japanese surrendered when we were two days off the coast of Canada. There was great hilarity in their portion of the ship, singing and guitar playing and much merriment.

"The food aboard the ship was superb and the menus something we could only imagine had existed after being on war-time rations for so long. This was the first trip the ship had made since before the war. It was a beautiful ship, spotlessly clean and in wonderful condition. It was an uneventful crossing in beautiful weather.

"The first stop was St. John's (Newfoundland) to allow some war brides to disembark. Then we sailed to Halifax. This was another traumatic experience, as I had to give up Johnie to an army officer and a Red Cross nurse to be taken to his father. I hope Johnie had a happy life with his father.

"Because of the influx of troops coming home at that time who were transported by CPR, we were put on CN trains and sent north. We saw nothing but trees and lakes. Not a living soul along the way, only fishing shacks along the lakes. There were only war brides and children on the train. When we got closer to inhabited areas, little towns, etc., the locals would come and wave to us. Sometimes the train would stop and some of the girls would run to a store to buy fruit or candy. We arrived in Winnipeg, Friday, August 18. There were only a few of us left on the train by this time. We were met by Red Cross representatives. Only two of us went on to Brandon.

"Unfortunately, I would miss the train in Brandon to take me to Glen Ewen, Saskatchewan, by two hours. The conductor phoned ahead and held the train so

continued on page 92

Newly arrived wives get help from a Canadian official. For many of them, arriving in Canada was a bewildering experience. Not all the husbands were able to return to Halifax to greet their war brides. Quite a few women had to travel with their children across a vast country. For an English-born woman, the magnitude of travelling by train from Nova Scotia to a homestead in Saskatchewan must have seemed overwhelming.

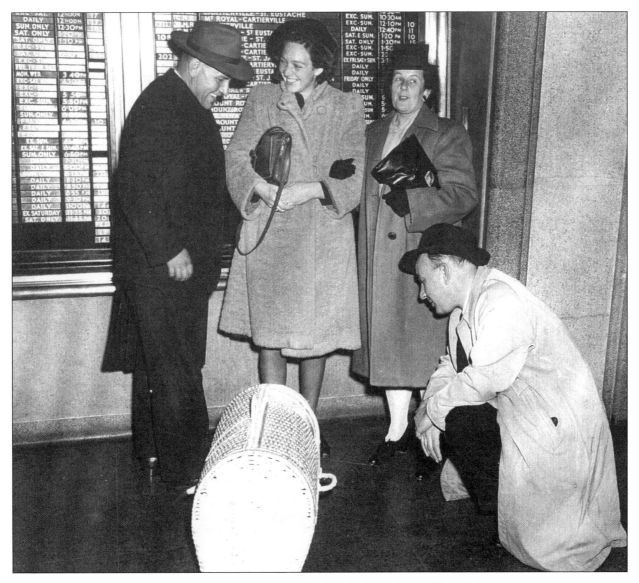

Two war brides and their Canadian husbands, dressed in civilian clothes, inspect a basket, similar to ones used by the Dutch immigrants as cradles for infants.

I would not have to stay in Brandon waiting for the next train, which was scheduled for Monday. I was impressed with the Canadian's tolerance and kindness towards us. I was glad to see my husband in military uniform at the station because I had never seen him in civilian clothes.

"I would not like to live anywhere else. I have been happy in Canada. I raised four children here who have been an asset to their community. It is a great country and I have always admired Canadian people. I am a member of the Saskatchewan War Brides Association as well as the Alberta War Brides Association. We enjoy our reunions and we have a bond that can't be broken. It is an unusual friendship that we have.

"I would just like to close by saying the Canadian boys that went overseas to aid in the conflict gave up their youth and had to face situations that were not normal for men of their age. There will never be a body of men like them again. The war brides love the veterans and have been honoured to share their country and their way of life on farms, rural settings that were foreign to us."

Mini (Hoogenkamp) Porter, of Overysel, Holland, remembers so vividly the Nazi invasion during World War Two:

"It was horrific. For approximately five years, we had to be in the house by 8:00 p.m. or by 6:00 a.m. No lights were to be on at night. My father was sent to Berlin, Germany, to a slave labour camp. When my father was allowed to come home for short leaves, my girlfriend's father would take his place in Berlin. My father was finally released from the slave labour camp because he was so sick.

"[Sundays] were good. We were allowed to go to town, which had long streets and little cafés. All the young people, including myself and my girlfriend, would go to town. We had fun."

In 1945, Mini met and started dating Allan Porter, a Public Relations Officer for the Canadian Government War Office. He was from River Hebert, Cumberland County, Nova Scotia. "I could hardly speak any English but Allan helped me and I also found some books so I could learn to speak the language. Allan and I married shortly afterwards then he returned to his duties.

"We had a baby boy and I'll never forget that the Red Cross sent parcels filled with baby clothes. In August 1946, myself and our son, left Rotterdam on The Lady Rodney, which sailed to England. We joined up with other war brides and

their children. We left England on the Queen Mary and sailed to Pier 21. I was so seasick but everybody helped to take care of our son.

"We arrived at Pier 21 and the staff and volunteers welcomed us so warmly and helped us with our papers, luggage, etc. I remember we were given fudge, something I had never eaten before. Allan's mother and brother met us at Pier 21.

"We decided to stay overnight in a hotel in Halifax. Our son was in a wicker basket (made in Holland) that had a top on it. The taxi driver, thinking it was part of our luggage, put the basket—baby and all—in the trunk and closed it. We still laugh about that today.

"The next day, we travelled to my new home in River Hebert. I was the only war bride in that small town. At first, I was very lonely and the language difference didn't help. But everyone was very helpful and very accepting of us. I remember making bread for the first time in my life. The family would be coming home from the mines and they were hungry. I had so much dough and I didn't know what to do with it, so I buried most of it in the garden!" (Mini Porter).

Georgina [Ena] Haynes— "The war brides boarded The Lady Rodney in England sailed for Pier 21 in Halifax. We were one day out of Halifax, our ninth since we left England— everyone was getting excited again. We had to wash our hair and get in shape for docking at the Pier. With three hairdressers on our deck, we could have our hair done—no trouble—just wait your turn. It was quite a shock when my shampoo wasn't making suds and after the rinse, my hair seemed stiff when dry. We had forgotten that our toilet water was not fresh, but salt. What laughs we all had!

"Once in Halifax, we ventured on deck, but we didn't see too much—a few lights from the city. When daylight came, everything was busy again. 'Call to the Purser's desk for the Maritime Brides.' This didn't mean much to me until they said 'Brides for Nova Scotia and Prince Edward Island first.' There were three for Nova Scotia, one for PEI. Then a line-up at the Pier to get our money exchanged. We got quite a bit—over $4 for our English pound.

"As my eyes wandered, oh! What a surprise. My husband and his father, both in uniform, were waiting to greet me. My husband was allowed on board, to my joy. I passed him my bag to carry and when I saw him with it afterwards, was quite relieved when I knew it hadn't been opened. We were allowed to leave Pier 21 and visit Halifax while waiting for the train to take me to my new home. The stores, to me then, were out of this world. So many things to buy and what a time I had when I did buy a gift to send back to my mother."

These women and their children are part of a group of war brides who land-ed in Halifax on board the SS *Scythia* on March 26, 1946 on their way to the British colony of Newfoundland. They are, from left to right, Mrs. H.R. Stone, Labrador; Mrs. Guy Frazer, St. John's; Mrs. A.J. Brown, baby Lawrence and David, St. John's; Mrs. Jean Day and son Peter, Trinity Bay; and Mrs. Marion House and daughter Marion, Saint Barbe.

Dorothy Powell— *"Just a brief story of my meeting with my smashing Canuck. I was a member of the WAAF and I heard from an old school chum of mine that she was to marry a Canadian and could I get leave to attend the wedding.*

"I did obtain leave and returned to Manchester for the wedding. The night before the big day, we went to the station to meet her fiancé (Russ) and his dad, who also served. Well, Russ also brought a pal of his to act as best man as his brother couldn't make it. His brother (Ted) turned up the next day and his pal (Ron) spent the rest of his leave with me. We kept in touch for the next few years and when he returned from Italy, we married on July 31, 1945.

"I had to wait for release from the air force before coming to Canada. I sailed on The Lady Rodney on May 24, 1946, and arrived at Pier 21. After several months of living in Canada, people kept asking if I liked living here and I would always say, 'I'll tell you when I've been here for four seasons.' Needless to say, I stayed."

Mary Radden met her Canadian merchant mariner in Bristol, England, at the George Railway Hotel where she worked, and married him six weeks later on June 6, 1941. A.B. Randolph Canning was a merchant mariner from Nova Scotia who served on the *Kai Koura* from 1940 to 1941 and then on the *Balt Rover* from 1941 to 1943. Mary, a step-dancer from Lisdoonvarna in County Clare, Ireland, explained why the ceremony took place so quickly: "We grabbed at any chance of happiness in our lives during the war. We thought we were all going to die."

Randolph Canning left the Merchant Marine in 1943 to join the RCMP Marine Division. He served aboard the *Irving*, *Wood*, *Steel*, and *Blue Heron*, and remained with the RCMP until his retirement.

Mary, as a war bride, sailed with her two daughters Eileen Perry (Canning) and Theresa Redid (Canning) aboard the H.M.T. *Mauretania*. On December 14, 1944, clutching her national registration identity cards (needed because of their age), Mary and her daughters arrived at Pier 21 to be greeted by her husband and an immigration officer—the first two to come aboard. Later she told her daughter Eileen, who had only been a baby at the time, about arrangements on board: "All the troops were above us. The war brides and children were not allowed to go up where the troops were."

Mary and Randolph settled in St. Margaret's Bay and later moved to Parrsboro, Nova Scotia, where they lived with Randolph's mother, to whom Mary was devoted. She told her daughter that the day the war ended, "I cried all day long. I thought of all the horrors we had lived through in England and I thought of my family in Ireland."

Mary returned to Ireland in 1966 to visit her family. She and Randolph raised four children in Canada before their deaths, about ten years ago. All through her life, Mary Canning stoutly maintained that, "The Canadian servicemen were the most thoughtful, reserved, respectful patrons that they had ever served. They never complained. They were very caring and asked for nothing."

Edna Perry (Dobbin) was a war bride from Newfoundland, then still a British colony. In 1940 Felix Perry, like so many of his contemporaries, enlisted as a soldier with the West Novas. Private Perry boarded a train for Halifax and Pier 21 where he was shipped to Newfoundland in August 1941 aboard the *Sydney Queen*, part of a convoy of some 31 ships and one destroyer. In Newfoundland, he met and later married Edna Dobbin. The young couple had only a few months together before he was sent on a driver's training course in Woodstock, Ontario. Then, in November 1943, he was shipped overseas with three hundred other soldiers on the Polish ship the *Chrobry*. After arriving safely in England, the soldiers were sent to Scotland for further training before being sent into action on the battlefields of Italy. He records: "No training had prepared me for the horror on the battlefield…Canadian and German bodies everywhere…Sometimes the screaming and crying drowned out gunfire and falling bombs."

It was while he was at the front that he received some good news, however, in a letter from Edna in which she announced: "our baby was born the night before last. I've called her Mabel Margaret."

In 1945, with the war over, Felix Perry cabled Edna that he would be arriving at Pier 21 with the West Novas aboard the S.S. *Pasteur*. She quickly replied, "Dear Felix, Mabel and I will be counting the hours, Love Edna."

It wasn't quite as simple for Edna as it seemed. As Newfoundland was not a part of Canada at that time, she was technically a war bride and needed a baptismal certificate for both herself and her daughter to be presented at Pier 21. Nonetheless, Edna kept her promise. As the S.S. *Pasteur* docked, Private Felix Perry looked around for his war bride and child. His son Felix (LeRoy) Perry recalls him saying, "This little girl ran and jumped into my arms with only the word 'Daddy.' It was the happiest moments of my life."

War Brides Song
(Composed by War Brides aboard The Lady Rodney*)*

Oh! The drums bang and the symbols clang,
And the war brides lead the way.
It's forward into Canada, you can hear them say,
We all hail from a mighty country,
To a lovely one we go,
To our dear Canadian husbands,
The smashers we used to know.

We left the town of Southampton,
On the 15th day of May.
Then upon the Rodney, we were all feeling gay,
We left the shores of Blightly in the afternoon that day,
And some of the girls were crying,
Hurrah, we're on our way!

We're feeling fine — that's a very good sign,
Our spirits rule the day,
To us it's simply home from home
The old Canadian way.
Where ere we go from east to west,
We want you all to know,
We'll make the best Canadians,
No matter where we go.

—Donated by a visitor to Pier 21

In 2000, war brides from across Canada met, many for the first time in over 50 years, and held a reunion at Pier 21. They toured Halifax Harbour aboard the HMCS *Preserver* as guests of the Canadian Armed Forces.

War brides, accompanied by crew of HMCS *Preserver*, walk down the gangplank.

Two war brides from New Brunswick dance together dockside. HMCS *Preserver* is in the background.

Group picture of the Canadian Red Cross (c. 1920s). Over the years, the Red Cross worked tirelessly to help immigrants. Before World War Two, they set up a nursery for children of weary immigrants. During the war, they packed boxes of food, clothing and other supplies to accompany the troops serving in Europe. And after the war they continued their work, helping the British, who were struggling with post-war shortages, by packaging "Boxes for Britain."

CHAPTER EIGHT

Pier 21's Distinguished Voluntary Organizations

"It was the kindness in her voice that made me notice her above the noise in the station. 'You look so tired,' she said. 'Would you like some help?'"
—Inge Vermeulen, German Immigrant

Whether in wartime or in peacetime, at both Pier 2 and Pier 21, volunteers worked tirelessly to welcome new arrivals, reassure them, answer their questions and help them with their documentation. They soothed querulous children, gave young parents a needed break, provided food, drinks, and a quiet chat. They spoke many languages and offered their services as interpreters to frightened newcomers struggling with papers written in English. They attended to the sick and cheered detainees whose paperwork was not in order or who were likely to be deported. Whether they were dealing with troops on their way to or returning from war, British guest children, evacuees from war-torn Europe, war brides, refugees, or immigrants, volunteers were pierside to greet them.

Volunteer organizations included the Sisters of Service (SOS), the Catholic Women's League, the Knights of Columbus, Port Chaplains, a number of clerical organizations, the Imperial Order Daughters of the Empire (IODE), the Red Cross, and the Young Women's Christian Association (YWCA). Many an immigrant recalls the kindness of these volunteers.

Sisters of Service

"It was the kindness in her voice that made me notice her above the noise in the station. 'You look so tired,' she said. 'Would you like some help?' Who was this woman? She was dressed in a long gray cotton outfit with a gray and white headdress that looked like a cross between a bonnet and a nun's wimple. Was she a Canadian nun? A Roman Catholic nun? 'Let me take the little ones to the nursery while you go to the waiting-room and have something to eat.' She was moving along with the children and some luggage while I followed with the rest of the bags, still wondering what do. As much as I appreciated her help I had to be honest and tell her the truth about us. 'We are Protestant,' I whispered. She laughed. 'You are people who need a hand, aren't you?' A Catholic nun looking after the children of Protestant immigrants—it was beyond anything ever encountered in my native Germany. Was this CANADA?" (Inge Vermeulen, German Immigrant).

The Sisters of Service (SOS) was founded in Toronto in 1922 for the purpose of welcoming Catholic immigrants to Canada, providing religious and spiritual support, and assisting them in their integration into Canadian society.

On September 5, 1925, three Sisters arrived in Halifax at the invitation of Archbishop Edward McCarthy. They were to "welcome, assist, direct, and care for all Catholic immigrants arriving in Canada through Pier 2." And they stayed through until Pier 21 the latter closed its doors in 1971.

The Catholic Women's League agreed to sponsor the sisters and the Honorable Nicholas Meagher, Judge of the Supreme Court of Nova Scotia,

97

Nova Scotia Baptist Federation volunteers assist new immigrants at Pier 21.

Christmas at Pier 21 for the children newly arrived in Canada. Many of these children were from war-torn Europe and had never enjoyed a Christmas party.

donated his home at 42 Morris Street as a residence for the sisters and "for the purpose of conducting a hostel for immigrant girls." Groups that helped them with their work included the Catholic Women's League, Knights of Columbus, Port Chaplains, various clerical organizations, the IODE, and the Red Cross, among others.

Within a month the sisters were hard at work. In their first report to headquarters, they wrote: "We have been present at the arrival of fifteen ocean liners and the nationalities represented were British, Germans, Italians, Americans, Polish, Russians, Romanians, Norwegians, Swedes, Maltese, French, Czechoslavs, Finns, Syrians, Jews, Hungarians, Dutch and Yugo-Slavs."

The hostel at Morris Street was a residence for British girls who immigrated under the "assisted passage" program, set up by the federal government. The program found domestic work for a year for new immigrants. The sisters acted as an employment bureau, offered support and counselling, and provided a place to go on the girls' days off. They offered a program of social, educational, and religious activities that soon attracted young women from rural Nova Scotia as well. The mix of Canadian and British women provided the new immigrants with a chance to socialize and make friends with Canadians their own age.

During World War Two, the hostel was particularly busy as many young women flocked to Halifax to take over jobs previously carried out by men. They worked in factories, as conductors aboard trams, or delivering the post. They may have done the work of men, but they certainly didn't receive the pay of their male colleagues.

The sisters were a welcome sight at Pier 21. As each liner berthed, they greeted passengers, often in their own languages. They reassured the new immigrants, interpreted for them when dealing with immigration and other officials, located lost luggage, sent letters back home and telegrams to relatives in Canada, bought train tickets and food for train journeys ahead, gave directions and information, even provided ethnic newspapers and magazines. Before the trains pulled out of the stations, the sisters would go from coach to coach, making sure the passengers were comfortable. And they would visit and offer whatever assistance they could to those unlucky enough to be housed in the detention quarters, because of illness or incomplete immigration papers.

The sisters also provided a critical "referral service." They obtained the names, addresses, and destinations of all immigrants listed on the ships' manifests and mailed this information to the chancery offices and parishes where newcomers were to settle. This service was a vital link that connected immigrants with churches in their new homeland.

The outbreak of World War Two in September 1939 brought immigration to Canada to a near standstill. There was still some work for the sisters as they comforted British guest children and other evacuees and refugees who made their way to Halifax. But Pier 21 and the port of Halifax were under the jurisdiction of the Department of National Defence and wartime security measures were in place. Many of the services offered by the sisters had to be curtailed. Yet they continued to walk troops to their ships, offering compassion, comfort, and reassurance.

With the end of the war, the sisters were busier than ever, dealing with returning troops, war brides and their children, and the exodus of refugees and displaced persons. With their fluency in other languages, sisters such as Dulaska, Kelly, and Jansen were able to reassure new immigrants, including a number of young displaced persons sponsored by the Canadian Department of Labour to work under contract for one year.

Until the 1970s the sisters could be found at Pier 21, while Dutch farmers arrived in the late 1940s and 1950s, Italian immigrants in the 1950s and 1960s, Hungarians fleeing the Soviet Union in 1956-57, and, in 1967, Czechoslovakians escaping uprisings in their country. Angelo Bolotta arrived at Pier 21 from Italy in 1955, as a five-year old child. She remembers Sister Salvatrice Liota:

"As a child, I remember vividly my arrival at Pier 21 in 1955 along with my mother. My sources tell me that you, Sister Liota, are one of the few remaining Sisters of Service who worked at Pier 21. I remember fondly that one of the first Canadians I met was you who introduced me to Kellogg's Cornflakes…the total immigrant experience cannot be told without explicit reference to the important role that the Sisters played in welcoming and assisting new immigrants.

"This is one immigrant's way of saying thank you to all Sisters of Service for helping to make the adjustment to life in Canada easier for many of us. Through our collective efforts, Canadians old and new have built the 'best country in the world.'"

Kellogg's cereal manufacturer provided cartons of corn flakes for newly arrived immigrants, many of whom had never seen packaged cereal before. Unclear about its use or food value, they would discard their packets.

Just a few of the boxes of supplies the Red Cross packaged and sent overseas during the war years. The soldiers often shared their supplies with besieged Europeans.

Often the floor of Pier 21's reception area was littered with corn flakes and packaging.

The Canadian Red Cross

The Canadian Red Cross and its volunteers were on hand when Pier 21 opened its doorways in 1928. One of their first undertakings was to set up a nursery for immigrant children. They would take the children, bathe them, and dress them in clean clothes donated to the Red Cross. Babies were settled in cribs with cots beside them for their mothers, while the rest of the family was fed. The nursery operated 24 hours a day and must have been a welcome relief for harried mothers.

The Red Cross continued its work during World War Two. Volunteers packed food, clothing and other supplies in boxes that were shipped overseas with the troops leaving Pier 21. Even today, there are Europeans who fondly remember the troops and those boxes. Chris van Valburg, a boy in Kersteren, Holland, during the Nazi occupation, recalls receiving supplies: "The Canadian troops would share everything they received from the Red Cross with us less fortunate in Holland and all over Europe." Even after the war, the Red Cross was there with the other voluntary organizations. They continued to pack boxes for overseas, now called "Boxes for Britain," to help the people of post-war Britain struggling with food and clothing rationing. They were also there to greet the war brides, refugees, and displaced persons who flooded to Canada in the late 1940s and throughout much of the 1950s.

"We came in February with no winter clothes or rubbers, and our little girl was very hungry…we immediately were given hot cocoa and cookies….As long as I live I'll never forget how good those cookies tasted" (Latvian refugee).

Imperial Order Daughters of the Empire

The volunteers of the Nova Scotia chapters of the IODE made a significant contribution both to the war effort and to Pier 21. They looked after the children of immigrants who landed at Pier 21 while papers were being checked and also helped immigrants find their trains.

During the war, they saw the troops off, supplying them with several amenities. Others greeted returning troops or prepared meals. A few women ran a canteen at Pier 21 for the soldiers. There was a similar canteen in the Civic Building in Truro, which provided troops in transit a place to eat, write letters, and socialize. Those letters were very important. Barb Clark, a child during World War Two whose mother was a member of the IODE chapter in Amherst, recalls the postmen who had to deliver the letters. Those letters meant a lot to the women and many a postman good-naturedly endured the wrath of a woman who did not receive a letter.

Some of the women collected good leather gloves and painstakingly took them apart, stitch by stitch, to remake into vests for the Canadian Merchant Marine. One such vest, found recently in an attic, has been donated to the Maritime Museum of the Atlantic, where it is on display.

The IODE also raised large amounts of money very quickly. They were able to purchase a Bolingbroke Bomber (stored in Ottawa, with talk of perhaps restoring it one day) and two fighter planes—one destined for England, the other for Australia.

A plaque at Pier 21 recognizes the contributions made by the women of the IODE during World War Two and the help they offered immigrants, war brides, and their children after the war.

The Young Women's Christian Association

The Young Women's Christian Association (YWCA) was involved with immigrants to Canada throughout the twentieth century. Members saw troops off to World War One and greeted them on their return. The organization helped victims deal with the catastrophe of the Halifax Explosion in 1917 and worked through the Depression years to ease suffering. From 1935 until 1945, the YWCA housed, entertained, and helped as many people as possible. They met returning troops off ships or trains, found accommodations for single women, helped the war brides and their children, and took care of many of the British evacuee children. They set up special clubs for the wives of servicemen and provided them with a nursery school and baby clinic. A second clinic was arranged for refugees and displaced persons arriving after the war. In 1988, the YWCA and the war brides held a reunion.

Leather vest made by IODE volunteers by taking apart leather gloves and sewing them together. Very few of these vests survive. This one, in such good condition that it may never have been worn, was found in an attic and was donated to the Maritime Museum of the Atlantic.

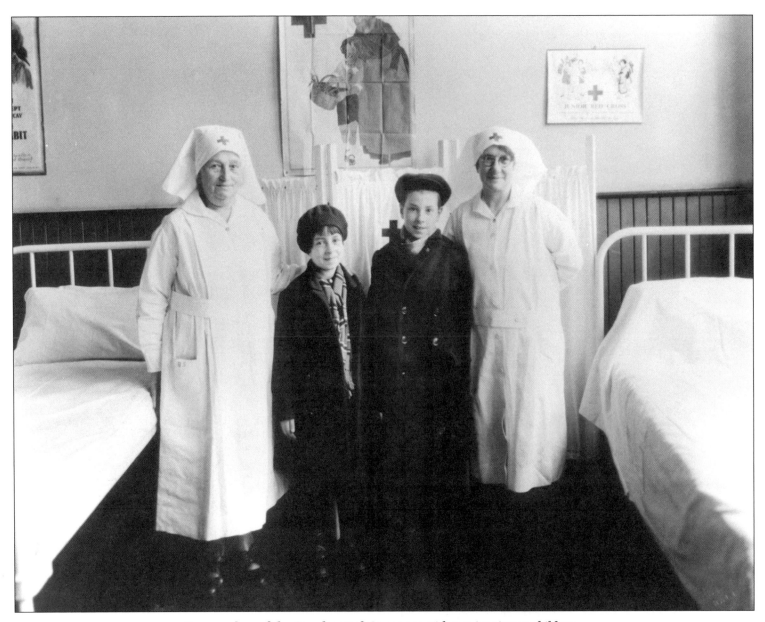

Two members of the Canadian Red Cross pose with two immigrant children.
One Latvian refugee never forgot the hot cocoa and cookies the Red Cross
worker gave her and her young daughter.

Red Cross nurses with immigrant mothers and children at Pier 21 (c. 1948).

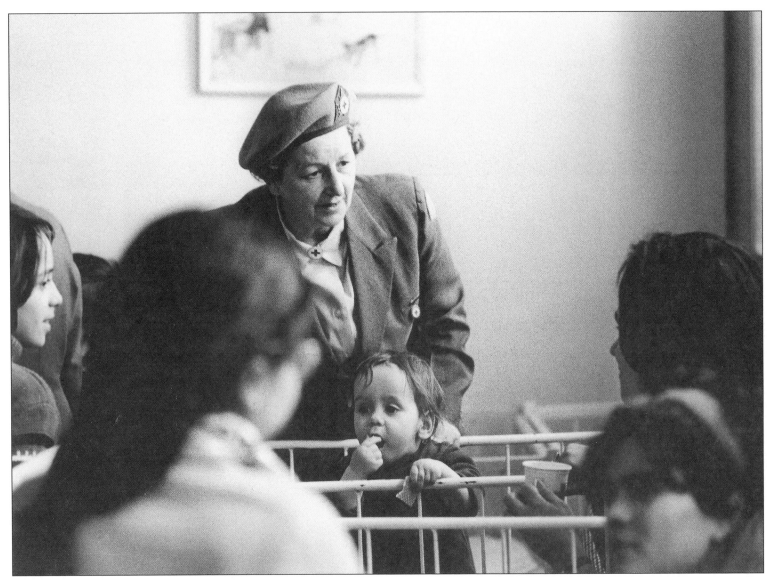

IODE member helps out at the nursery at Pier 21. Processing newly arrived immigrants took time. They had to undergo medical examinations, document verification, and interviews with immigration officers. Volunteer organization members often took care of children while their parents went though the process.

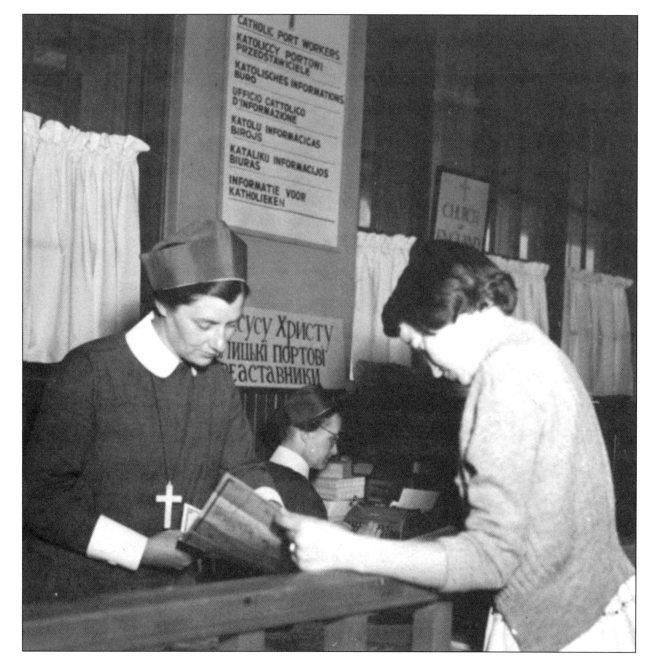

The Sisters of Service were a mainstay on the Halifax waterfront since 1925. Over the years they opened a hostel for immigrant girls. During the war years, they comforted weary soldiers. And in the post-war era, they were always on hand to greet passengers in their own languages, help them through immigration, and provide a referral system so that parishes would be informed of impending new arrivals and be ready to welcome them. Here, one of the sisters staffing an information booth helps a new immigrant while behind her on the board are notices in a number of different languages (c. 1950).

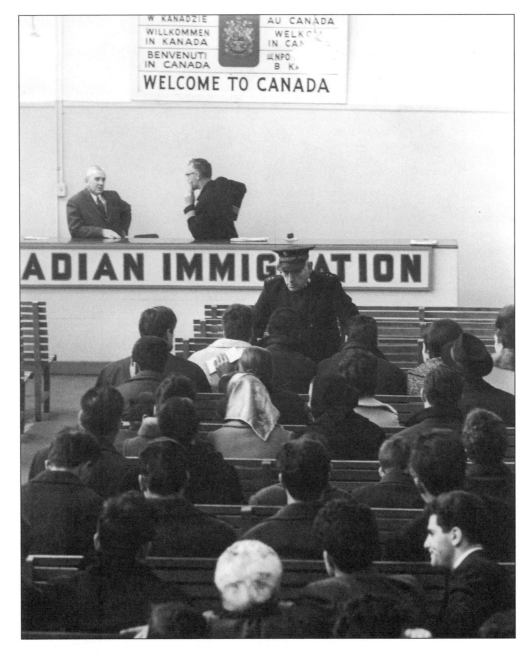

Immigrants await processing.

CHAPTER NINE

Refugees and Displaced Persons —The Post-war Years

"There are things of which I may not speak,
There are dreams that cannot die;
There are thoughts that make the strong heart weak,
And bring a pallor into the cheek,
And a mist before the eye."
—Henry Wadsworth Longfellow, "My Lost Youth"

The plight of refugees in Europe began before the start of World War Two. The rise of Fascism in Germany, Austria, Italy, and Spain drove millions from their homes long before war was declared on September 3, 1939. Marianne (Echt) Ferguson wrote about her experiences in pre-war Poland in 1942, when she was just 16. She and her family fled to England aboard the Polish ship *Luvow* on February 16, 1939. After four days they boarded the *Andania* and sailed for Halifax and Pier 21, where Mrs. Ferguson is a volunteer.

"Those words from Longfellow have more meaning for me than for most people…To me those words mean that I have seen and experienced so much during my childhood in Danzig (Poland) that the things are hard to speak of, because they have been so horrible; but the memory cannot die, and yet, it makes me sad to think of them. And even in such a country, a country of tyranny, barbarism and hatred, people have dreams of freedom and liberty, which may come true to some of them.

"We had our dreams come true. Like a sunbeam from a clouded sky, came permission for us to come to Canada, a free country.

"Things had been going from bad to worse for the people who were against the Nazis. Here where everybody is free, one does not realize just how terrible it
is to be ruled by a dictator. Danzig was called a free city, but it was under the authority of both Germany and Poland, although some things were controlled by Danzig itself. However the majority of the population of Danzig was German and thus, Hitler thought he could dare to control more of Danzig that he should.

"We, ourselves, had a very nice home and beautiful garden. In the summer our friends and relatives from the city visited us every day, and we all went to the beach, which was only a little way from our house. We used to take our lunch with us and stayed till evening or we went walking in the park. Later on, when Hitlerism was more advanced, Jews and anti-Nazis were not allowed in the park and on most places on the beach.

"When things became too unbearable, we decided to leave the country, and we were very fortunate in getting a permission to come to Canada. We sold most of our things, but many we packed and sent to Gdynia, Poland, from where we sailed to England.

"We left Danzig in February 1939 and stayed in Gdynia for ten days before we sailed away. Many of our friends came to see us in Gdynia and many of our old friends in Broesen told us not to leave. One woman, whom we met on the street in Danzig just before we left, said loudly: 'All the good people leave and the bad ones stay.'

A Hungarian refugee is helped by an interpreter from the Department of
Immigration. Thousands of Hungarians managed to escape the Russian invasion of their homeland in 1956 and made their way to Canada, often with little or no documentation and only the clothes they carried with them.

"On February 16th, 1939, we sailed to England on the Polish liner Luvow. *There we stayed four days and then we boarded the steamship* Andania *and sailed to Halifax. In Halifax we were welcomed by a lady who brought us to a hotel where we stayed eight weeks. We were constantly looking for a farm with the help of some very nice people who have become our very good friends. We bought the farm on which we live now and are much happier here then we were in Danzig. Of course, we work hard, but we have our freedom and that is better than living in a country of slavery. We do not wish to go back to Danzig because we like Canada very much. It is a land where all people have equal rights, where everybody may worship in his own way and where all people are free. May it always be so, and may no dictator ever have a chance to set foot on Canadian soil."*

The aftermath of World War Two left many civilians in Europe destitute and homeless. Some were from countries under Communist rule such as Poland, the Ukraine, Hungary, Yugoslavia, and Latvia. Others were from countries that had yet to recover from the war, including Italy, Austria, and Hungary. Those who could not get back to their home countries were known as Displaced Persons or DPs. Those who came from countries still suffering the ravages of war, whose homes and livings had been destroyed, came to Canada as refugees.

Approximately 100,000 displaced persons and refugees steamed into Pier 21 in the years following the war. Most were destitute and frightened. Often they arrived with little more than the clothes on their backs—no passports, no birth certificates, no official documentation, no money and no sponsors. They came in boats barely fit for passage, such as the *Capry*, which arrived in Halifax with 23 Latvian and five Estonians on board. These desperate people had used the last of their money to buy an old British gunboat that had been abandoned in Sweden. As one official at Pier 21 stated: "Their acute despair was evidenced by a species of fright, which even the kindness of train officials were unable to allay."

Some of the stories of these displaced persons and refugees are harrowing. In 1947, word was received in Canada that a small boat, *The Walnut*, was being made ready by refugees from one of the Baltic countries to sail to Canada. The 347 refugees on board began a three-week odyssey in 1948, which brought them to Sydney, Nova Scotia. There they were sent on to Halifax, sailing into the harbour on December 18, 1948. Immigration officials certified 300 of them.

They were soon followed by another 2,400 refugees fleeing the Soviet Union—none of whom had proper documentation. While the Canadian Government grappled with the limitations of existing immigration laws, church groups and other organizations soon lobbied for these Soviet refugees to be allowed to stay in the country even if they didn't meet regular immigration regulations. Even so, some failed to be certified as landed immigrants and had to await a hearing, an appeal, or deportation. One immigration official wrote: "the motives for deception were not selfish. A harried father who had managed to keep his tattered family intact until now would have been driven to deception by a desperation borne of love for his dependents."

The Sisters of Service stepped in and appealed to the public for the establishment of a fund to be distributed among refugees so that they could buy food and train tickets. And Haligonians threw a Christmas Eve Party and Christmas Day celebration. In January and February 1949, the Soviet refugees were relocated to an employment centre. Today they and their descendants live in the Toronto area.

In August 1949, the *Sarabande*, an old minesweeper, arrived in Halifax with 238 DPs—including 60 children—from Poland, Latvia, Estonia and Finland. Many had been branded while incarcerated in German and Russian concentration camps. They were admitted to Rockhead Quarantine Hospital until permitted entry to Canada. All were accepted as landed immigrants.

Saddest, perhaps, were the Jewish survivors of the Holocaust. Jewish displaced persons, refugees, and orphans were not welcomed to Canada, despite entreaties by the international community and Canadian officials working in Europe who recognized the desperation of the Jewish refugees. A member of the Canadian team of the United Nations Relief and Rehabilitation Administration in Europe wrote as follows to the Minister of Health and Welfare. "I wish Canada would offer to take a group of Jewish children. So far no country has offered any permanent haven to any of them. Canada says it must play the part of a major power. Well let her show herself. Let her be the first to offer refuge to some of these children. We have here thousands of orphans all of whom have no place to go. I can't tell you what it would mean to thousands of people to think that at long last one country had offered to take even a small group of children. I would absolutely burst with pride if Canada were to offer a home to some of Hitler's victims. It would be a magnificent gesture."

A priest passes out food to new immigrants aboard a CNR coach. The immigrant trains did have dining cars, but many new immigrants, especially refugees, could not afford a catered meal.

Despite the difficulties, the Jewish Immigrant Aid Society (JIAS) worked tirelessly to ease the plight of European Jews arriving in Canada. Society members, such as Sadie (Fineberg) Morris, who spoke seven languages and volunteered at Pier 21 for four decades, welcomed immigrants from all nations. The plight of European Jews, during and after the war, is best summed up by Fraidie Martz, who recalls: "Ever since I could remember—and long before the war—I had been awakened from sleep by my parents' agitated talk…about terrible things that were happening to fellow Jews in Europe…my mother and father believed they could shield me from their fears…."

In January 1949, about 17 Jewish orphans, ranging in age from ten to eighteen, arrived at Pier 21. They had escaped and were either living in the wilderness or under non-Jewish names until they could flee. On arrival, they were cared for by the JIAS and the local synagogue before moving on to Montreal to be adopted by new families.

In time the Canadian Government came to recognize fully the needs of these people. The War Orphans Project of 1947-49 was the first major child welfare program and test case. Under it, 1,100 orphans and 15,000 Jewish refugees were allowed entry to Canada. The International Refugee Organization (IRO) and the JIAS paid passage for each young orphan. In the meantime, the Canada Jewish Congress worked with various agencies to find homes for them, as well as clothing, food, education, and medical care for them. It was a difficult project but in the end it met with success.

Another group of children, this time Polish, underwent a terrifying odyssey as they were harassed from Europe to North Africa, and back to Europe again, always with the Polish Government barking at their heels. Many of their parents had been deported to Russia and they were alone. The IRO learned of their plight and put them aboard the *General Heitzelman*, bound for Halifax. At Pier 21, they were met by an IRO officer who welcomed them with compassion. One Latvian refugee remembers clearly receiving the help of just such an officer: "We came in February with no winter clothes or rubbers and our little daughter looked very hungry and miserable. The IRO officer took us into his office and sent out for something warm to drink and something to eat."

In 1950, the Canadian Government changed the Enemy Alien Prohibition Act, which developed from an arrangement for the immigration of German nationals. Security regulations were kept tight so that neither Nazis nor Communists would be allowed into Canada.

Tony Sosnkowski arrived at Pier 21 as a refugee on board the *Batory* on July 13, 1940:

"We sailed from Gourock in Scotland under a very powerful convoy escort, which included no less than the battleship HMS Rodney. Much later, I found out the reason for all that naval protection was not us refugees but British gold bullion being shipped for safekeeping for the duration of the war.

"I have been deeply grateful all my life for the warmth and kindness of our reception and the care, education and even affection which we received."

Laszlo Galambos, a Hungarian refugee, wrote of his arrival at Pier 21 on February 16, 1957:

"My first feelings about Canada, Halifax and the New World were a mixture of confusion, terror and curiosity. While on board the Britannic waiting to dock, I became aware of the requirement that upon arrival we were to be taken to a 'hall.' To my Hungarian ears that notion sounded unusual. You see, in Hungarian, 'Hal' with one 'L' means 'fish'—so I imagined that we were all to be taken into a giant fish! And the smells upon arrival at Halifax did not do much to convince me otherwise."

For Elsa Taurens Dwyer, a Latvian refugee who arrived January 23, 1949, the train ride across Canada was particularly memorable:

"My strongest memory of the train ride is looking out into the night, seeing nothing but snow covered fields, with small groups of houses here and there, brightly lit and inviting through the darkness. As we passed through small towns or over level crossing, the locomotive whistled. The sound was mournful and scary, but at the same time exciting. Even now, whenever I hear a train whistle, I am instantly reminded of my first glimpses of Canada."

The landscape viewed from the train also made an impression on Robbie Waisman, a Jewish war orphan who arrived on December 3, 1948:

"On the trip west, I couldn't get over the immensity of the huge spaces and sparse settlements along the way. You could see forever. As I crossed Canada by train, it occurred to me that so many people could have been saved in this vast country. So much land and yet no room for Jewish refugees during the war."

Refugee mother and child 1950s.

For travel-weary mothers, the sight of the Red Cross and its nursery must have been welcome indeed. Many immigration ships arrived at night, which meant that children had to be awakened to disembark. Volunteers took babies and young children, bathed and fed them, then placed them in cots or cribs to sleep while their parents went through the immigration process.

This mother with her baby and young daughter await disembarkation. Often when there was a crush of immigrants, some individuals and families had to remain onboard until others had been processed. Whenever possible, priority was given to families with young children.

CHAPTER TEN

New Immigrants

"the gangplank is now tied to the pier...the immigrants start the long procession...they are from every part of Europe... The newcomers to Canada are from all stages of life."
—Father Anthony Des Lauriers

Refugees and displaced persons were not the only ones to enter Canada through Pier 21 in the years following World War Two. Canada, in better economic shape than many European countries, opened its doors to immigrants, especially skilled workers from Great Britain, Western Europe, and the United States, reaching a peak in 1948 when over 60,000 people arrived in the country.

These post-war immigrants were well prepared. They had their papers in order and they brought their possessions and savings with them, though some countries placed restrictions on the amount of cash an individual could leave with. In Holland, for example, each adult could bring $100 and each child, $50—hardly enough to start a new life. Many Dutch used their savings to buy possessions, which they sent to Canada in wooden boxes. It was said that many Dutch brought everything—including the kitchen sink.

Of the many nationalities that mingled on the ship gangplanks at Pier 21, Father Anthony Des Lauriers wrote: "the gangplank is now tied to the pier...the immigrants start the long procession...they are from every part of Europe: the Baltic, the Black Sea, Ukraine, countries behind the Iron Curtain, Italy, Brittany, Holland, England, Austria, Belgium. The newcomers to Canada are from all stages of life."

In the post-war years, Canada underwent an agricultural crisis. So many farmers and farm workers were leaving for better opportunities in the cities that many farms were abandoned. Immigrants with the skills to make those farms profitable again were eagerly welcomed. The Land Settlement Act, created to assist Canadian farmers, was amended in 1948 to offer assistance to immigrants on the same basis as other Canadians.

Many of the new immigrant farmers were Dutch. Holland had been devastated by the war and much of the good farmland, reclaimed by Dutch dykes, had been destroyed as the Nazis systematically sabotaged the dykes and dams. Those with farming experience were sponsored to come to Canada and remain on a farm for one year, being paid about $100 per month plus room and board. After a year, they would be able to take out Canadian citizenship and apply for an interest-free loan to purchase their own farms.

For one young bride, Hendrika Los, the sea voyage aboard the *Beaverbrae* in February 1950 was less than she had hoped for: "The ship was not a luxury liner, nor was it a honeymoon cruise for Jake and I. It was a huge disappointment. You were not able to buy anything on board. But even more disheartening were the sleeping arrangements. Jake and I had separate sleeping quarters. Jake slept in the front of the ship and I slept in the middle of the ship. I slept in a large room with approximately 90 other women and children. What a honeymoon!"

The Dutch were not the only immigrants to take up farming in Nova Scotia. But all seemed to be successful, according to the Nova Scotia Farm

Dutch immigrants in the hall (reception area), waiting patiently to be processed. Immigrants from Holland arrived in great numbers in the years following World War Two, perhaps in part inspired by a country that they considered to be their liberators. But the Government of Nova Scotia also actively recruited Dutch immigrants to take over farms because many young Canadians were flocking to urban centres, leaving behind family farms.

Mother and son ready to disembark at Pier 21.

Loan board, which wrote: "It is interesting to note that the loans of immigrants were all in good standing in 1954. The immigrants that established themselves on farms proved to be good citizens, rapidly adapted themselves to their new environments and in many cases made valuable contributions towards improved conditions in the districts they settled."

Italian immigrants began to arrive after 1948, sailing on such ships as the *Cristoforo Columbo* and the *Leonardo De Vinci*, often to be greeted personally by the Italian Vice-Consul to Canada. In one year, approximately 30,000 Italian immigrants first stepped onto Canadian soil at Pier 21. Among them was Irene Ursano's family. Ms. Ursano wrote: "My mother (29 years of age) and my brother (nine years of age) arrived at Pier 21 in late December 1952 from Italy. They were met at Pier 21 by the Sisters of Service with gifts as Christmas had just passed."

Many immigrants, although not classified as refugees or displaced persons, still arrived penniless. In 1951, Konstant Trus arrived at Pier 21 after a ten-year odyssey to freedom from the Ukraine, a country that after suffering under Nazi occupation was then a part of the Soviet Union. Mr. Trus remembers the poverty of his family upon arrival at Pier 21. "Except for the clothes we wore," he wrote, "we were without money and possessions."

There were other destitute immigrants: those whose sponsoring families failed to appear, who had no money and no job to go to, who often spoke little or no English. Many, such as art curator and German immigrant Robert Dietz, remained at the Pier 21 immigration quarters while they worked at manual jobs, such as clearing snow off the rail lines, or looked for permanent work. Wrote Mr. Dietz: "...we were happy, we had shelter, food and kind and friendly immigration officers. We felt protected, sheltered, not jailed" (December 12, 1951).

Canada continued to welcome the disenfranchised, including 18,000 Hungarians who fled the uprising of 1956 and arrived at Pier 21 on such ships as the *Ivernia, Carinthia,* and the *Cascania.* Like so many other immigrants over the years, they brought with them a unique culture that has helped to enrich this country.

By the end of the 1960s, Pier 21 was no longer needed. The jet airplane had replaced the ocean liner and most immigrants arrived in this country at an airport, not at a seaport. The Department of Manpower and Immigration could not justify the expense of Pier 21.

The last group to arrive were Cubans. They had flown to Gander, Newfoundland, seeking refugee status. Since obtaining visas could take up to six months, 100 of the Cubans were transported to Pier 21 to be accommodated. For the staff, they were a joy to have around now that immigrant ships no longer docked. The new refugees introduced staff and volunteers to the delights of Cuban cuisine and remained through Christmas.

Pier 21 closed its doors in March of 1971 after more than one million immigrants and soldiers had passed through its doors. For those who worked and volunteered there, it was the passing of a way of life: "with the closing of Pier 21, a chapter of Canadian life was finished. Pier 21 was in many ways a bustling self-sufficient village hidden within the vast anonymous looking transit shed. The people who worked there will never forget it."

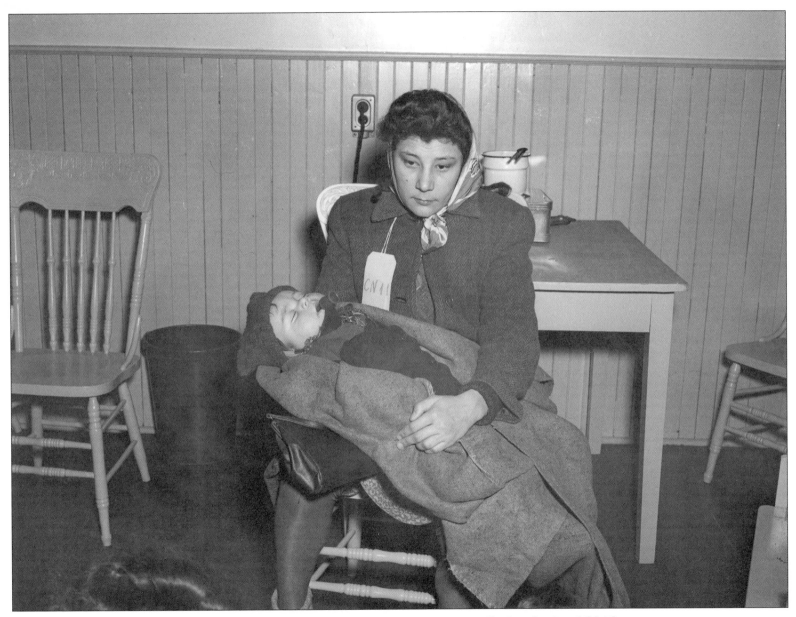

An immigrant mother, looking weary after a long sea journey, cradles her sleeping child. The tag attached to her collar suggests she is partway through the immigration process.

This 1950s photograph shows the waiting area in the reception hall, where immigrants awaited processing. It's not hard to imagine it teeming with immigrants from all over Europe.

These wire cages were an issue of contention among staff at Pier 21. Many thought they looked unfriendly—and indeed frightening—to immigrants who had left behind a war-torn Europe. Hand luggage was kept in the cages until immigrants could collect theirs, but in 1956 the port manager was convinced that a luggage counter would be just as effective and less imposing.

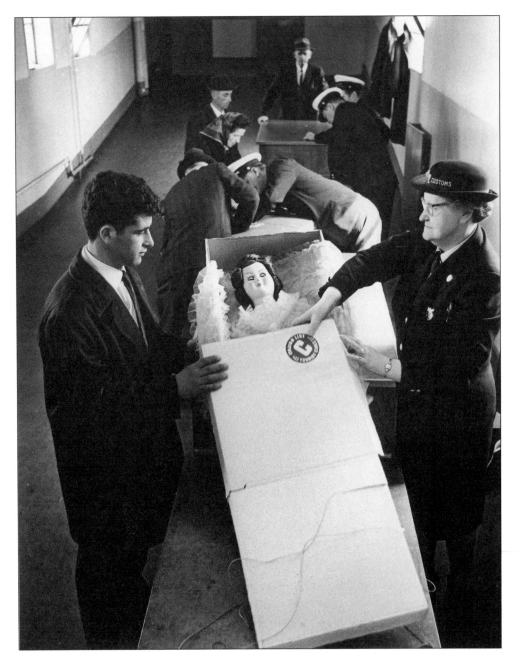

Two customs officials check luggage. All kinds of items were not allowed to be imported into Canada for health or other reasons, including various foodstuffs, animals, and even wood shavings used to protect furniture.

S.S. *Olympia*, **one of many post-war immigrant ships, docked at Pier 21.**

The newly refurbished entrance to Pier 21. The train beside the steps, partially hidden by snow, is typical of the post-war trains that took new immigrants to other parts of Canada. The train is not open to the public.

CHAPTER ELEVEN

Pier 21 Today

"Yesterday I toured Pier 21 and stood on the deck where my father left for Europe and returned to Canada during World War Two. My tears dropped to the floor where he stood in line...almost sixty years earlier."
—Oral Carswell Ritchie

The Pier 21 Society

One in five Canadians has a direct connection with Pier 21, making it a very important part of the history of Canada. The Pier 21 Society was formed by a group of Haligonians determined to preserve this living piece of history. The mandate of the Pier 21 Society is to transform Pier 21 into a facility of international importance, acknowledging the significance of immigration to the building of Canada and the strength of our cultural diversity. During the early stages of the society's formation, one thing became clear: no matter what the future held for Pier 21, it would always remain in the hearts and memories of the people who had arrived here. As board members shared their ideas of what Pier 21 could become, they heard from people who had returned to Halifax, almost as a pilgrimage, tracing the paths they had taken when they first arrived in Canada.

The first president of the society was John Paul LeBlanc, a career public servant in the Department of Employment and Immigration who helped renew interest in this former immigration shed and created the first Board of Directors. Regretfully, Mr. LeBlanc died on January 26, 2002 as this book was being completed.

In 1993, Ruth M. Goldbloom became the second president of the Pier 21 Society. Under her direction, the board initiated a feasibility study followed by a business plan to make Pier 21 a reality. Then in 1995, at the end of the Halifax G-7 Summit, Prime Minister Jean Chretien elated members by announcing that as a legacy to the host city, the Federal Government would provide a $4.5 million pledge towards the re-opening of Pier 21, provided the society raised matching funds.

A National Advisory Committee and an Atlantic Committee, led by Ruth Goldbloom, were struck; they began telling the story of Pier 21 and its significance to Canada in boardrooms and homes across the country. In May 1997, a national fundraising campaign was launched with over $1 million worth of commitments announced. The private sector continued to respond with gifts of various sizes and, by 1998, the full $9 million had been raised. In November of that year, work on the site began; it re-opened eight months later on July 1, 1999, as a high-tech interactive facility. Today, the executive and board of the Pier 21 Society are responsible for the operation of Pier 21, although the ultimate success of Pier 21 continues to depend on a strong volunteer component.

Sherry Porter, the new chair of Pier 21, states in Pier 21's newsletter "Passages":

"We have had a great season of programs. Heritage Day celebrations were delightful, very well attended and hopefully the start of an annual tradition we

As visitors enter the facility on the lower level, they pass between two walls of brick, each brick with the name of an immigrant who passed through Pier 21.

Immigrant luggage came in all shapes and sizes—from the small, austere suitcases handed out by CORB to the British guest children to larger steamer trunks. Immigrants carried hand luggage with them but larger items were stored in steel cages until immigration officials had inspected them. Care was taken to make sure that undetected immigrants, such as foreign insects or mites hidden in straw used for packing, were not admitted.

Left: Two visitors investigate some of the items in a typical immigrant's suitcase. In addition to personal clothing and hygiene items, many immigrants carried in suitcases family treasures, such as photographs, jewellery, letters and diaries, or prized heirlooms.

Pier 21 has innumerable displays of passports, photographs, letters, post-cards, and official paper-work, collected over the years.

can celebrate our rich diversity…On March 26, 2001, Pier 21 was the launch site for the "Our Canadian Millennium Quilt." The quilt was co-ordinated by the Parc Downsview Park and was created by over 500 students from across Canada to celebrate Canada's historic and geographic diversity at the start of a new millennium. The Pier 21 Board, volunteers and staff continue to prepare for the future with strategic planning and create a national foundation, have fundraising initiatives, and educational programming and research…each day brings new and wonderful stories from those that passed through the portals of Pier 21 between 1928 and 1971 that help explain how we have become such a diverse and rich country."

Pier 21 has hosted conferences such as the Atlantic Jewish Council and International Day of the Lebanese Immigrant. Veterans such as those who served in the Canadian Merchant Marines, Canadian Forces and RCMP have toured Pier 21. Pier 21 works closely with veterans to foster greater awareness and appreciation of its past and present roles in Canada. Just how much the pier means to those who passed through its doors is evidenced by a donation: "The most touching moment of the evening was when one of the delegates thanked me for making this one of the most memorable evenings in his life. The look on his face said it all—he had arrived at Pier 21 from Germany fifty years ago as a child. This was clearly a return for him" ("Passages," Winter 2001-2002).

A series of programs, some of which are animated, also help develop a deeper appreciation of the courage and sacrifice many Canadians made. Pier 21 continues to host numerous visiting school classes as well as other special interest groups. Many phone calls and bookings are being made as Canadians discover this jewel of our national heritage, housed at this unique facility. Television stations such as the Canadian Broadcasting Corporation and RAI Television from Italy have filmed documentaries at Pier 21. The Kenneth C. Rowe Heritage Hall is ideally suited for corporate luncheons, elegant receptions, meetings, banquets, parties, and conventions. Guided tours are provided for an unforgettable tour of a chapter in the nation's history.

Pier 21 has always had a strong volunteer presence. Whether representing religious organizations, medical services, translators, the goal was—and still is—to make the new arrival feel comfortable and welcome. Sister Adua Zampese, who worked with Sister Salvatrice Liota at Pier 21 in the 1960s, writes of her return visit to the pier in August 1999:

"From the time I entered the pier, I felt in touch with my own experience of my arrival at the port with Sergio, my brother, in February 1957 on the la Motonava Saturnia. It would take me pages to relate to you my feelings. I know that my experience is not unique.

"I believe that what I say to you conveys the feelings that seeing Pier 21 evokes in the hearts of all of you, the SOS, other volunteer organizations, the staff, who all helped and supported us on our arrival in Canada. Here I was back at Pier 21—42 years later and in my heart still holding the feelings of that time long ago. As these waves of memories passed before me, I looked around and saw Pier 21 as it stands today. I was deeply touched at seeing the extent to which Canada went in transforming the inside of Pier 21 as they did, and in making it a living memory to the many immigrants who came to Canada through its gates. When I stood before the huge stand with pictures of SOS helping at the Pier, and when I saw other memorabilia and statements displayed at the Pier…I relived that day at the Port. What a consolation to find someone who spoke your own language, someone who would counsel, console, help and prepare the newly arrived for the rest of their journey into the new country. I remember seeing you helping the families at the customs, either translating or interpreting for them with the customs' officers. How well I remembered my introduction to sliced bread at my arrival in Halifax….I remember the kindness, the smiles, the loving care and concern for all newcomers. I knew what it meant to find a friendly person on our first day, days, and years in a strange land.

"Take what I am saying as coming from one who came, as an immigrant, through Pier 21, knowing no English, with pain in my heart, even if with much faith and hope for the future, as each newcomer carried within themselves. I will never forget the first people who welcomed me in Canada, the ones that accepted me, and who made me feel valued and that I belonged."

Pier 21's legacy has grown beyond Halifax. Last October, the first major fundraiser outside Nova Scotia was organized by members of the Italian community in Toronto, in collaboration with CBC and Telelatino. A part of the event was "Footprints on the Pier," a collection of stories and oral histories of immigrants who gave so much to Canada that took place in Woodbridge, Ontario and was recorded by the CBC ("Passages," Winter 2001-2002).

Pier 21: The School Program

Schools in Nova Scotia are encouraged to bring their students to Pier 21 and participate in the Pier 21 School Program. Upon arrival students are introduced to the history of facility before beginning their tour of the Rudolph Peter Bratty Exhibition Hall. A volunteer plays the role of an immigration officer while the students act the part of immigrants. They try to answer the questions that would have been asked of all immigrants who passed through Pier 21.

Pier 21 believes it is important that future generations understand the immigrant contribution and appreciate the multi-cultural country in which they live. Tours provide hands-on-learning opportunities to students so they may develop a deeper appreciation and understand of the role of Pier 21 in Canada. Information on school tours, rates and the Pier 21 passport program can be obtained by calling 902.425.2320 or by sending an e-mail to info@pier21.ns.ca.

Educational kits, the most recent being "Pier Into Your Past: A Family History Resource and Activity Guide," are published with support of the Historical Foundation and include information on sources used by genealogists.

Wall of Service

On the World War Two deck at Pier 21 is the Wall of Service, a permanent installation dedicated to the Canadian Armed Forces and the sacrifices made by members of the Royal Canadian Navy, the Canadian Army, Royal Canadian Air Force, Royal Canadian Mounted Police, and the Canadian Merchant Navy. It is a fitting tribute to the 500,000 men and women who left from Pier 21 to serve overseas, as well as those who returned and the 70,000 war brides and their children.

Oral Carswell Ritchie wrote about how he felt, standing on the spot where his father had embarked for Europe:

"Yesterday I toured Pier 21 and stood on the deck where my father left for Europe and returned to Canada during World War Two. My tears dropped to the floor where he stood in line with a jubilant group of teenaged boys, off to see the world, almost sixty years earlier. I felt how he must have felt, and was moved with overwhelming emotion at the memory of his circumstance. He was 32, older than most. He had experienced the pain of the loss of his first wife and baby in childbirth. He had recovered and married my mother, who was now seven months pregnant, and who would be very much alone and filled with the uncertainty of his fate. How would things go? Would he return? I once asked a war

buddy of my father's what my father was like overseas. He said 'He wasn't much of a mixer.' This surprised me to no end, as everyone knew him, and he was so friendly to everyone in town. He hated the war and everything to do with it. He just wanted to come home; to be at home with his wife and new family.

"I'm sure he couldn't avoid feelings of loneliness and despair, knowing the German U-boats were waiting for them as they crossed. He told us how they had converted the Queen Mary into a troop carrier. He had a hammock with a hundred others strung up in the swimming pool that had been drained to accommodate them. The ship was only five years old but held over ten thousand men, in makeshift accommodations. But my father was fortunate. He returned uninjured to his wife and the three-year-old boy that he had never seen, uninjured, but nevertheless was traumatized from his experiences. We often heard how my mother's feet 'flew' to greet him, and have the letters to diary their thoughts during those incredible years. I felt my father's joy and relief to disembark at Pier 21 and to be back home again."

Rudolph Peter Bratty Exhibition Hall

This self-guided interpretive centre was designed to allow individuals to trace the path an immigrant would have followed upon arriving at Pier 21. A multimedia presentation, audio and video clips, and numerous exhibits bring the immigrant experience to life. The Secunda Marine Wall of Ships is also located in the exhibition hall. There is a re-creation of a ship's funnel in the main display area. Also included are photographs of over 100 ships that docked at Pier 21.

A popular stop in the exhibition hall is the Bell Canada Ship Database, one part of a much larger information database containing immigration records, catalogued stories, and archival photographs. Individuals can look up the ship that brought them or their relatives to Canada. The database is upgraded continually. The hall may be booked for special events by contacting heritagehall@pier21.ns.ca, or visiting www.pier21.ns.ca. Catering services are available for dinners of up to thirty and receptions of up to 600 people.

In the Andrea and Charles Bronfman In-Transit Theatre enjoy a 25-minute virtual projection, "Oceans of Hope," which portrays the in-transit experience of all who passed through Pier 21 and the role it played for over forty years.

The main exhibition area on the second level has displays of paraphernalia donated by immigrants or their families.

Two visitors settle into coach seats in a simulated railway car. The trains that carried immigrants were well appointed with comfortable and clean coaches and small cabins that could be booked for those who could afford them. The display includes examples of the cramped but efficient quarters in the cabins.

The "train" with coach seats and cabins on one side, offers windows across the way through which one can watch moving images of Canada from the east to the west coast. The "train" shakes and rattles as it clatters along the tracks, and toots its horn as it passes over railway crossings or enters towns.

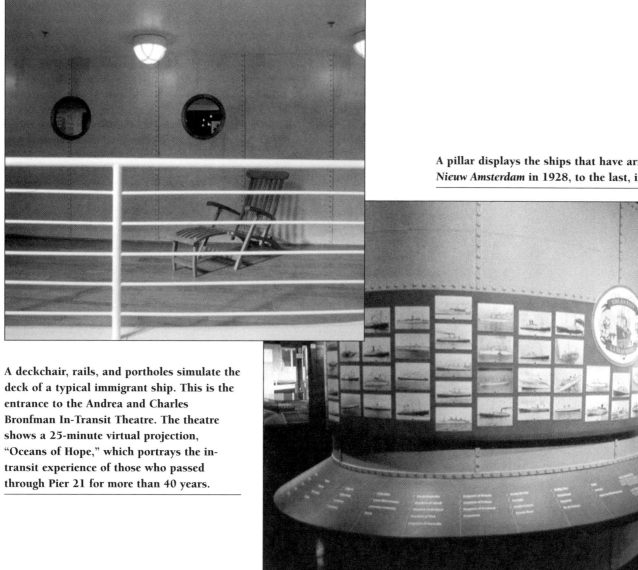

A pillar displays the ships that have arrived at Pier 21—from the earliest, the *Nieuw Amsterdam* in 1928, to the last, in 1971.

A deckchair, rails, and portholes simulate the deck of a typical immigrant ship. This is the entrance to the Andrea and Charles Bronfman In-Transit Theatre. The theatre shows a 25-minute virtual projection, "Oceans of Hope," which portrays the in-transit experience of those who passed through Pier 21 for more than 40 years.

The observation deck with a telescope to view Halifax Harbour. On a good day, a visitor might be able to see a cargo ship approach one of two city shipping terminals, or a tugboat edging an oil tanker to the Dartmouth Refinery. In summer, pleasure crafts, tour boats, and huge luxury cruise liners that tie up along piers 20 and 21 can be seen. But there are no longer ships teeming with immigrants or bringing war weary troops back from Europe.

A volunteer animator plays the role of an immigration officer while school children pretend to be immigrants and answer the questions of all visitors to Pier 21.

Reconstructed immigration office. Here travellers would have waited their turn to present passports and immigration papers.

Library and Resource Centre

The resource centre houses a wealth of information valuable to individuals at Pier 21, their descendants, researchers, historians, school groups, and other interested parties. It includes unique images compiled from valuable sources such as National Archives of Nova Scotia, many of which are on display in the exhibition hall. The collection also holds newspaper photographs, the Allan S. Tanner Collection of images depicting Canadian troops and war brides returning to Pier 21, the Francis E. Murphy Collection, which documents the building of the piers, and donations of various images by other individuals. There are other donations of ships and books, including a growing collection of books on topics relevant to Pier 21, such as Canadian immigration and the Canadian military in World War Two.

The centre houses photographs of approximately 90 per cent of the ships that brought people to Halifax between 1928 and 1971. There are also videotaped immigrant interviews, news coverage of Pier 21 and documentaries on Canadian immigration. Pier 21 also has a large collection of personal recollections of immigrants, war brides, refugees, troops, British guest children, staff, and volunteers.

Arrangements to visit or do research through the resource centre may be made by contacting the research librarian at library@pier21.ns.ca

Gift Shop

The gift shop offers a wide choice of multi-cultural and international books and gifts as well as souvenir items with the Pier 21 logo.

For further information—

Please check Pier 21's web site at:
www.pier21.ns.ca
You can also write:
Pier 21, 1055 Marginal Road, PO Box 611, Halifax NS B3J 2R7
Phone: (902) 425-7770
Fax: (902) 423-4045

The Pier 21 stamp, published as part of the
Millennium Collection postage stamps.

The gift shop, just outside the entrance to the Pier 21
exhibition space, offers a wide range of memorabilia
and Nova Scotian crafts and books.

ODE TO PIER 21

Unimpassioned, I am no longer the Pier 21
of wooden ships and ocean liners,
Of barred windows, wire cages, and prison cells.
I gave way to the jet aircraft.
Hushed, abandoned, postponed,
I stand the husk of bygone days.

Silent, I am the platform that processed
Kings, queens, princes and paupers,
Intrepid pioneers, immigrants,
The detainees, inadmissibles,
Lost souls, penniless, the threadbare,
Those with USA destinations.

The torpedoed, refugees from tyranny,
Oppression and revolutions -
Displaced peoples - each
Sought land, hope, harmony, liberty.
War Brides. I greeted them all.

Ships of all descriptions conquered the ocean,
In Halifax Harbour, calm waters hugged their keels,
Soothing the spirit of their passengers.
Pouring from them they peopled the land.

I salute national heroes off to war,
Sailors, soldiers, airmen,
Both men and women - merchant seamen,
Those at rest at sea, in unknown and
Imperial War Graves, in Flanders Field.

I want to become the Pier 21
With walls that speak out.
I want to recall the hustle and bustle,
Of officials and volunteers,
Helpful hands. Dockhands, the longshoremen,

Counseling words and smiling eyes -
The Sisters of Service, the Red Cross, Religious groups,
The nursery. The cafeteria,
Red Caps, Aid to the traveller, and
Welcoming ambassadors and rail stop delegations.

My international landmark
Welcomed passenger boats, to-day cruise ships.
My plaque and interpretive panel,
Commemorate my history of national significance.

My guests gave Canada growth, nationality and diversity.
With generosity of spirit and in kind
They contributed to devastated Europe.
Heritage is my emblem of world understanding.
A visit is ennobled, the future bright.
To foster common ground is my vision.

John LeBlanc - 1995

Image Sources

Canada Post Corporation: 138 (left)

City of Vancouver Archives: 50

Cole, Sally: 81

Darrow, Paul: 95

Gentleman's Magazine: iv

Gates, Graham: 72

Halifax Port Corporation: 122, 123

London Illustrated News: 6, 7

Maritime Command Museum: Title Page, 2, 3, 20, 21, 24, 27, 29, 30, 33, 36(bottom), 37, 38, 39, 45, 47, 48, 49, 53, 54, 56(bottom), 57, 58, 60, 63, 68, 69, 84, 85, 86

Maritime Museum of the Atlantic: 82

Miscellaneous Private Collections: ii, 5, 12, 15, 17 (bottom), 25, 34 (top), 40, 71, 73, 87, 101

Nimbus Publishing: 17

Nova Scotia Archives and Records Management: Cover, 8, 10, 11, 13, 14, 18, 19, 22, 23, 36 (top), 52, 55, 66, 74, 75, 76, 93, 105, 106, 121, 125

Pier 21: 16, 26, 28, 34 (bottom), 42, 46, 51, 59, 62, 64, 67, 79, 88, 90, 91, 96, 98, 99, 104, 108, 110, 112, 114, 115, 116, 118, 119, 124, 133 (top), 135 (top), 136 (role-playing), 138 (right)

Sisters of Service: 107

Thompson, David: 32, 103, 126, 128, 129, 130, 133 (bottom), 134, 135 (bottom), 136 (office), 137

van de Wiel, Debi: 56 (top)

Walker, Harry: 44